THE
Mauna Loa®

MACADAMIA
COOKING
TREASURY

D1197602

THE

Mauna Loa®

MACADAMIA COOKING TREASURY

Leslie Mansfield

CELESTIAL ARTS
Berkeley, California

Copyright ©1998 by Leslie Mansfield. All rights reserved.
No part of this book may be reproduced or transmitted in any form
or by any means, electronic or mechanical, including photocopying,
recording, or by any information storage or retrieval system, except
for brief review, without the express permission of the publisher.
For more information, you may write to:

CELESTIAL**ARTS**

P.O. Box 7123
Berkeley, CA 94707
e-mail:order@tenspeed.com
website:www@tenspeed.com

Celestial Arts books are distributed in Canada by Ten Speed Canada,
in the United Kingdom and Europe by Airlift Books, in South Africa by
Real Books, in Australia by Simon & Schuster Australia, in New Zealand
by Tandem Press, and in Southeast Asia by Berkeley Books.

Cover design by Greene Design
Cover and food photography by Larry Kunkel
Cover and food photography styled by Veronica Randall
Text design by Greene Design

Printed in Hong Kong

Library of Congress Cataloging-in-Publication Data

Mansfield, Leslie.
　　The Mauna Loa macadamia cooking treasury / by Leslie Mansfield.
　　　　p.　cm.
　　Includes index.
　　ISBN 0-89087-885-4 (cloth). –– ISBN 0-89087-880-3 (pbk.)
　　1. Cookery (Macadamia nuts) I. Title.
　TX814.2.M33M36　1998
　641.6'45––dc21　　　　　　　　　　　　　　　98-16925
　　　　　　　　　　　　　　　　　　　　　　　　CIP

1 2 3 4 5 6 7 8 9 10 / 08 07 06 05 04 03 02 01 99 98

TO RICHARD,

my husband and best friend,
thank you for a life filled with adventure shared.

Acknowledgments

Deepest gratitude goes to my husband Richard, who has helped me with every step—his name belongs on the title page along with mine. Boundless love and appreciation go to my wonderful parents, Stewart and Marcia Whipple. Limitless thanks for all the encouragement and support to everyone at the Mauna Loa Macadamia Nut Corporation, led by the singular vision of J.W.A. "Doc" Buyers. I must single out Terry Inglett, President, his incomparable assistant Teresa Fraticelli, and Gary Carlson, Director of Retail, for their unflagging efforts and energy on my behalf. Very special thanks go my publisher David Hinds, without whom this book would still be just a great idea; to my editor, stylist and new best friend, Veronica Randall for her expertise, imagination and humor; to the wonderful Heather Garnos for being Veronica's right arm; to Brad Greene for a spectacular design; and to Larry Kunkel for glorious food photography. Thanks to Jan Cook at Stock Photos Hawaii and John Penisten for gorgeous Hawaiian photos; and Sally Furness at Floral Resources for the beautiful flowers. Many thanks also to Catherine Cavaletto, Associate Professor of the Department of Horticulture at the University of Hawaii, for her expert advice; Jeanne Herbst, Patrick Edie, and Gene Erger for recipe ideas, and to Deb Gatta for her help in a pinch.

Special thanks to Gage, my darling nephew and favorite recipe critic whose, "MMM! Auntie, that's good! My tummy's full!." always warms my heart.

Finally, this book would not have been possible without the cooperation of the many people who graciously contributed their favorite macadamia recipes. I wish to thank them all for their generosity.

There are two species of macadamias which produce edible nuts. One is the rough-shell macadamia, M. tetraphylla. The other, commonly known as the smooth-shell, goes by the botanical name M. integrifolia. Although both are grown commercially, most plantings are of the smooth-shell macadamia.

Contents

Introduction

Mention macadamias and visions of chocolate-glazed clusters of crunchy, buttery heaven come to mind. Although this tropical treat has become synonymous with Hawaii, it is also a versatile ingredient in both sweets and savories. Macadamias enjoy a greater availability than ever before and are being eagerly embraced by chefs around the world, who are delighted by their contribution of creamy flavor and smooth texture. The Mauna Loa® Macadamia Cooking Treasury *celebrates this versatility with dishes that are both foreign and familiar, traditional and exotic.*

Introduced from eastern Australia in the late nineteenth century, the commercial cultivation of the macadamia tree began in earnest in the 1950s when methods for cracking and removing the hard shell from the nutmeat were developed and perfected. Today, the finest macadamia orchards in the world climb the majestic slopes of Mauna Loa on the Big Island of Hawaii where the volcanic soil, abundant rainfall and equatorial sunshine provide ideal growing conditions.

Growing macadamias is a time and labor intensive operation. The trees begin to bear nuts at five years old, and don't reach their full bearing potential until fifteen years of age. The trees blossom periodically and yield nuts in waves, requiring five or six harvests annually. Mechanical harvesters collect roughly half the fallen nuts, but crews of hand-pickers are needed to harvest those in less accessible locations. With close to one million trees on ten thousand acres and decades of refining its orchards, Mauna Loa has earned its reputation as the leader in the macadamia nut industry.

‹STARTERS

PART I

Cream of Tomato Soup with Onion and Garlic Macadamias

The vitamin C from all the tomatoes combined with the generous contribution of garlic make this a marvelous winter meal when flu season threatens.

3 tablespoons butter

1 onion, finely chopped

3 pounds ripe tomatoes, peeled, seeded and chopped

2 tablespoons packed brown sugar

1 tablespoon minced fresh basil

1 bay leaf

1 teaspoon salt

$1/2$ teaspoon freshly ground black pepper

2 whole cloves

$1^1/2$ cups half-and-half

1 cup Onion and Garlic Macadamias, page 12

Snipped fresh chives, for garnish

In a large stockpot, melt butter over medium heat. Add onion and sauté until very tender. Add tomatoes, brown sugar, basil, bay leaf, salt, black pepper and cloves and stir well. Reduce heat to low, cover and simmer until tomatoes are cooked through, about 30 minutes. Remove bay leaf and cloves and discard. Purée soup in batches in a blender. Return puréed soup to pot and stir in half-and-half. Heat through over low heat, do not allow to boil. Serve topped with a sprinkle of Onion and Garlic Macadamias and chives.

SERVES 6

Caramelized Maui Onion, Goat Cheese and Macadamia Tartlets

The combination of sweet Maui onions, buttery macadamias, and tangy goat cheese creates a kaleidescope of taste sensations with every bite. If you can't find Maui onions where you live, be sure to use the sweetest onions available.

CRUST:

1 cup flour

7 tablespoons cold butter, cut into small pieces

1 egg yolk

1 tablespoon Mauna Loa Macadamia Oil

4 large Maui onions or other sweet onions such as
   Walla Walla or Vidalia, coarsely chopped

2 tablespoons water

1 teaspoon sugar

1/2 teaspoon salt

Freshly ground black pepper, to taste

6 ounces fresh goat cheese

20 whole Mauna Loa macadamias

For the crust: Place flour and butter in the bowl of a food processor and process until mixture resembles coarse meal. Add egg yolk and process just until mixture holds together. Flatten dough into a disc, cover with plastic wrap and chill for 1 hour.

In a large skillet, heat the oil over medium heat. Add onions, water and sugar and stir to coat with oil. Reduce heat to low, cover and simmer for 45 minutes, stirring occasionally. Remove cover and increase heat to medium. Cook onions, stirring often, until onions are a deep golden brown and liquid has evaporated. Season with salt and pepper and cool.

Preheat oven to 375 degrees F.

On a lightly floured surface, roll out crust to a 1/4-inch thickness. Cut out circles with a 3-inch round cookie cutter. Fit into 2-inch round tartlet tins and trim off excess dough. Place tartlets on a baking sheet. Fill each tartlet with 1 tablespoon goat cheese, 1 tablespoon caramelized onions and top with a whole macadamia. Bake for about 25 minutes or until pastry is golden brown. Cool for 15 minutes before removing tartlets from the tins. Serve warm.

MAKES ABOUT 20 TARTLETS

Eggplant Dip

This savory dip is much lower in fat than most, so serve it with a clear conscience and plenty of pita bread.

2 eggplants
1/4 cup lightly packed fresh Italian parsley leaves
1/4 cup chopped Mauna Loa macadamias
3 tablespoons freshly squeezed lemon juice
2 cloves garlic, minced
1 1/2 teaspoons salt
1/2 teaspoon freshly ground pepper
1/4 cup olive oil

Preheat oven to 375 degrees F.

Place whole eggplants on a baking sheet. Roast for 20 to 30 minutes, or until skin is blackened and eggplants are very soft. When cool enough to handle, cut off stem end. Slice into quarters lengthwise. Place skin side down on a cutting board. With the back of a knife, scrape the flesh off the peel. Discard the peel.

In the bowl of a food processor, combine the eggplant flesh, parsley, macadamias, lemon juice, garlic, salt and pepper and process until smooth. With motor running, add the oil in a thin stream until all is incorporated. Serve with pita bread.

MAKES ABOUT 3 CUPS

Spinach and Feta Triangles

I used to make this traditional Mediterranean dish with pine nuts until I discovered how much richness the macadamias added. I like to serve them with kalamata or my own home-cured olives.

1 tablespoon butter

1 onion, finely chopped

8 ounces fresh spinach, chopped

1/4 cup finely chopped Mauna Loa macadamias

1 tablespoon minced fresh parsley

1/2 teaspoon freshly ground pepper

8 ounces feta cheese, crumbled

1 pound filo dough

3/4 cup melted butter

Preheat oven to 400 degrees F.

In a large skillet, melt the butter over medium heat. Add the onion and sauté until translucent. Add the spinach and sauté until wilted and liquid has evaporated. Stir in the macadamias, parsley and pepper and sauté until macadamias start to turn golden. Remove from heat and place mixture in a large bowl. Stir in the feta.

Unfold the filo sheets. Use only 1 sheet at a time and keep the remaining sheets covered with a damp tea towel to prevent them from drying out. Lay one sheet on a cutting board. Using a pastry brush, brush the filo with melted butter. Lay a second sheet on top of the first, and brush with butter. Continue layering and buttering until you have used 4 sheets of filo. Using a sharp knife, cut the filo lengthwise into 3 strips. Place 1 heaping tablespoon of the filling at the center of the bottom of 1 strip. Fold one corner over to form a triangle. Continue folding over triangle to the end of the strip. Brush top with butter and place on a baking sheet. Repeat until all filo and filling are used.

Bake for 10 to 15 minutes, or until golden brown.

MAKES ABOUT 24

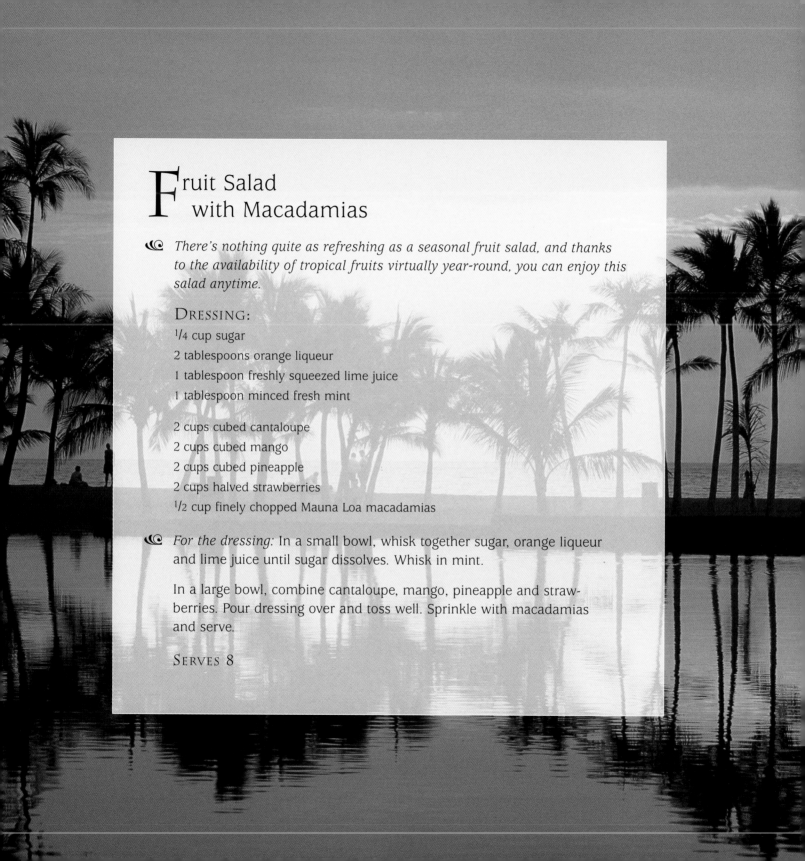

Fruit Salad with Macadamias

There's nothing quite as refreshing as a seasonal fruit salad, and thanks to the availability of tropical fruits virtually year-round, you can enjoy this salad anytime.

DRESSING:

1/4 cup sugar

2 tablespoons orange liqueur

1 tablespoon freshly squeezed lime juice

1 tablespoon minced fresh mint

2 cups cubed cantaloupe

2 cups cubed mango

2 cups cubed pineapple

2 cups halved strawberries

1/2 cup finely chopped Mauna Loa macadamias

For the dressing: In a small bowl, whisk together sugar, orange liqueur and lime juice until sugar dissolves. Whisk in mint.

In a large bowl, combine cantaloupe, mango, pineapple and strawberries. Pour dressing over and toss well. Sprinkle with macadamias and serve.

SERVES 8

Sweet and Spicy Pepper Nuts

This is a sophisticated nibble to serve with cocktails and makes a marvelous condiment to accompany an Indian curry or a Thai buffet.

1/4 cup butter

1/2 cup packed brown sugar

1 tablespoon water

2 teaspoons freshly ground black pepper

1 1/2 teaspoons salt

2 cups Mauna Loa macadamias

Preheat oven to 350 degrees F. Lightly oil a baking sheet.

In a large non-stick skillet, melt the butter over medium heat. Add the brown sugar, water, pepper and salt and stir to dissolve the sugar. Add the macadamias and cook, stirring often, until syrup thickens and turns a deep brown. Spread onto baking sheet and bake for about 10 minutes. Place baking sheet on a rack to cool. Break into small pieces when cool enough to handle. Cool completely and store in an airtight container up to 2 weeks.

MAKES ABOUT 2 CUPS

Onion and Garlic Macadamias

These are wonderful to snack on or serve as an appetizer. Try sprinkling them over salads and soups for extra flavor and unexpected crunch.

2 tablespoons butter

2 teaspoons minced dried onions

2 teaspoons dry parsley

2 teaspoons salt

1 teaspoon freshly squeezed lemon juice

1 teaspoon onion powder

1 teaspoon sugar

1/2 teaspoon garlic powder

2 cups Mauna Loa macadamias

In a skillet, melt butter over medium heat. Whisk in dried onions, parsley, salt, lemon juice, onion powder, sugar, and garlic powder until smooth. Stir in macadamias. Sauté about 5 minutes.

MAKES ABOUT 2 CUPS

Cinnamon-Sugar Spiced Macadamias

Be warned, this is one of my most requested recipes, so you may want to double the batch. It's easy and fun to make as a special project with the little ones for holiday get-togethers.

$^{1}/_{2}$ cup sugar

1$^{1}/_{4}$ teaspoons cinnamon

$^{1}/_{4}$ teaspoon ground ginger

$^{1}/_{4}$ teaspoon salt

1 egg white

2 cups Mauna Loa macadamias

Preheat oven to 300 degrees F. Lightly oil a baking sheet.

Stir the sugar, cinnamon, ginger and salt together with a fork until blended. Whisk in the egg white until foamy. Stir in the macadamias. Spread mixture onto the prepared baking sheet and bake for 10 minutes, stir and bake an additional 10 minutes. Cool and store in an airtight container.

MAKES ABOUT 2 CUPS

Sautéed Duck Livers on Grilled Macadamia Polenta with Tomato Coulis

The creamy duck livers are quickly sautéed and served on rich macadamia polenta, which is wonderfully complemented by the slightly acidic tomato coulis. Serve it as a decadent hors d'oeuvres or an elegant light meal.

TOMATO COULIS:

2 large ripe tomatoes, peeled, seeded and chopped

1 teaspoon freshly squeezed lemon juice

1 small clove garlic, minced

Salt and freshly ground pepper, to taste

GRILLED MACADAMIA POLENTA:

2 cups chicken stock

1 cup plus 2 tablespoons cornmeal

1/2 cup finely chopped Mauna Loa macadamias

2 tablespoons butter

Salt and freshly ground pepper, to taste

SAUTÉED DUCK LIVERS:

2 tablespoons butter

2 tablespoons olive oil

1 pound duck livers, trimmed and cut into bite-sized pieces

1 shallot, minced

2 tablespoons sherry vinegar

1/2 teaspoon sugar

1 tablespoon chopped fresh sage

Snipped fresh chives, for garnish

For the tomato coulis: In a small bowl, stir together all ingredients. Cover and allow flavors to meld for 1 hour.

For the macadamia polenta: Lightly oil an 8-inch square cake pan. In a heavy saucepan, bring the stock to a boil. Whisking constantly, slowly add the cornmeal in a thin stream. Continue whisking until mixture thickens, about

5 minutes. Reduce heat to low and cook, stirring often, until the polenta is smooth and thick, about 30 minutes. Stir in the macadamias, butter, salt and pepper. Pour the polenta into the prepared pan and cool completely.

For the duck livers: In a large skillet, heat the butter and oil over medium-high heat. Add the duck livers and sauté quickly until lightly browned on the outside but still pink on the inside. Remove the livers with a slotted spoon and keep warm. Add the shallot to the skillet and sauté until translucent. Whisk in the vinegar and sugar and deglaze the pan. Add the sage and whisk until fragrant. Remove from heat and set aside.

Prepare the grill. Unmold polenta onto a cutting board. Slice into 4 squares and brush on both sides with a little oil. Place on grill and cook until marked on both sides. Arrange grilled polenta on 4 serving plates. Top with sautéed duck livers and pour the pan juices over them. Spoon tomato coulis on top and sprinkle with chives. Serve immediately.

SERVES 4

Around the world, the macadamia is known by a variety of names. In its native Australia, the aboriginal name is the Kindal-Kindal. Other names include the Queensland nut, Bauple nut and the popple nut.

Butternut Squash Gratin

This is one of my favorite ways to prepare butternut squash. It makes a lovely side dish and even stands on its own as a delicious vegetarian entrée.

1 cup heavy cream

2 tablespoons minced fresh sage

1 teaspoon minced fresh thyme

2 cloves garlic, minced

$1/2$ teaspoon salt

$1/2$ teaspoon freshly ground pepper

1 small (about 2 pounds) butternut squash, peeled, seeded,
  thinly sliced and divided in thirds

6 ounces feta cheese, crumbled and divided in half

6 ounces mozzarella, shredded and divided in thirds

$1/2$ cup finely chopped Mauna Loa macadamias

Preheat oven to 325 degrees F. Lightly oil a $2^1/2$-quart baking dish.

In a bowl, whisk together cream, sage, thyme, garlic, salt and pepper. Set aside.

Place a layer of squash in the bottom of the prepared baking dish. Layer half of the feta and one third of the mozzarella. Add another layer of squash, then the remaining feta and one third of the mozzarella. Layer remaining third of squash. Pour cream mixture over the top of the squash. Sprinkle macadamias and the remaining mozzarella over the top. Bake for about 45 minutes, or until the top is browned and the squash is tender when pierced with a knife.

SERVES 8

Spaghetti with Gorgonzola and Macadamias

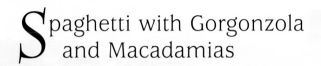 *When my husband put together a simple salad of wild greens and pears with this creamy pasta dish, he created a perfect first course that could easily moonlight as a light supper.*

2 tablespoons butter

2 cloves garlic, crushed

4 ounces Gorgonzola, crumbled

1/4 cup sour cream

3/4 cup finely chopped Mauna Loa macadamias

Salt and freshly ground white pepper, to taste

12 ounces spaghetti

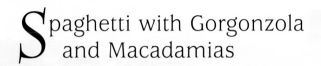 In a large saucepan, melt butter over medium heat. Add garlic and sauté until fragrant. Add the crumbled Gorgonzola and stir until melted. Add sour cream and stir to make a creamy sauce. Stir in the macadamias. Season with the salt and pepper.

Cook the spagetti in boiling salted water until *al dente*. Drain the spaghetti thoroughly, then add to the sauce in the pan. Stir gently until coated and serve immediately.

SERVES 4

Singapore Saté

This is Far Eastern fast food courtesy of the street vendors from one of my favorite cities in the world.

1 1/2 pounds flank steak, thinly sliced across the grain

MARINADE:
1 small onion, chopped
3 stalks lemon grass, pale tender part only, chopped
1 tablespoon chopped fresh ginger
2 cloves garlic
2 teaspoons sugar
1 teaspoon sambal oelek
1/2 teaspoon ground coriander
1/2 teaspoon cumin
1/2 teaspoon turmeric
1/4 cup soy sauce

MACADAMIA SAUCE:
1 tablespoon Mauna Loa Macadamia Oil
3 large shallots, minced
2 cloves garlic, minced
1 stalk lemon grass, pale tender part only, minced
1 teaspoon minced fresh ginger
1/2 cup unsweetened coconut milk
1/2 cup ground Mauna Loa macadamias
2 tablespoons freshly squeezed lime juice
2 tablespoons sugar
1/2 teaspoon fish sauce
1/2 teaspoon salt
1/2 teaspoon sambal oelek

For the marinade: In the bowl of a food processor, combine onion, lemon grass, ginger, garlic, sugar, sambal oelek, coriander, cumin and turmeric and process until smooth. With motor running, add soy sauce and process until well combined. Pour marinade into a shallow non-reactive dish. Add sliced beef and stir to coat. Cover and marinate in the refrigerator overnight.

For the macadamia sauce: In a saucepan, heat oil over medium heat. Add shallots, garlic, lemon grass and ginger and sauté until fragrant. Stir in coconut milk, macadamias, lime juice, sugar, fish sauce, salt and sambal oelek. Reduce heat to medium-low and simmer about 5 minutes. Remove from heat and pour into a serving bowl.

Prepare grill. Thread beef onto skewers and grill over hot coals for 3 to 5 minutes per side. Serve with macadamia sauce.

SERVES 10

*To toast macadamias,
preheat your oven to 350 degrees F,
place the macadamias on a
baking sheet and toast,
shaking the pan occasionally.
They should be lightly toasted
in about 7 minutes. Since they
burn easily, watch
them closely!*

Sweet and Spicy Glazed Chicken Wings

This ever-popular Chinese appetizer gets loads of extra crunch from the macadamias.

MARINADE:

1 cup lightly packed cilantro leaves

1/4 cup chopped fresh garlic

1/4 cup chopped fresh ginger

1 teaspoon dried red chile flakes

1 cup soy sauce

1/2 cup rice vinegar

SWEET AND SPICY GLAZE:

2 cups rice vinegar

1 1/2 cups sugar

2 teaspoons dried red chile flakes

1 clove garlic, minced

4 pounds chicken wings

3/4 cup finely chopped Mauna Loa macadamias

For the marinade: In the bowl of a food processor, combine cilantro, garlic, ginger and chile flakes and process until smooth. With motor running, add soy sauce and vinegar and process until well combined. Pour marinade into a large non-reactive bowl. Add chicken wings and stir to coat. Cover and marinate in the refrigerator overnight, stirring occasionally.

For the sweet and spicy glaze: In a saucepan, whisk together vinegar, sugar, chile flakes and garlic. Bring to a boil, then reduce heat to medium and simmer for about 25 minutes, or until mixture is reduced by half.

Preheat oven to 400 degrees F. Lightly oil a broiling pan.

Remove chicken wings from marinade and place on prepared broiling pan. Bake for about 20 minutes, or until done.

Place hot chicken wings into a large bowl, pour the hot glaze over them and toss to coat well. Sprinkle macadamias over and toss. Serve immediately.

SERVES 8

Brie and Macadamia Stuffed Mushrooms

I've had many variations of this recipe and knew it would be perfect with the addition of the macadamias.

1 pound large mushrooms, cleaned
1 tablespoon freshly squeezed lemon juice
1 tablespoon butter
1 tablespoon sour cream
1/4 cup finely chopped Mauna Loa macadamias
3/4 teaspoon salt
1/2 teaspoon freshly ground pepper
1/4 teaspoon fines herbes
4 ounces Brie cheese

Pull stems out of mushrooms and place mushroom caps on a broiling pan. Finely chop stems and toss with lemon juice. In a sauté pan, melt butter over medium heat. Add chopped stems and sauté until liquid evaporates. Stir in sour cream and sauté until mixture appears almost dry. Transfer mushroom mixture to a bowl. Stir in macadamias, salt, pepper and fines herbes. Let cool.

Trim the rind off of the Brie and discard the rind. Finely dice the Brie and stir into the mushroom mixture.

Preheat the broiler.

With a small spoon, fill the mushroom caps with the stuffing. Broil until bubbly and golden brown.

SERVES 6

Thai Corn Fritters

These feisty fritters can be served either warm or at room temperature as part of a Thai buffet, as a light lunch all on their own or as a zesty side dish with your favorite cut of steak.

$^1/_2$ cup all-purpose flour
1 teaspoon baking powder
1 teaspoon baking soda
1 teaspoon sugar
2 eggs, beaten
3 cloves garlic, minced
1 tablespoon fish sauce
1 tablespoon red curry paste
2 cups corn kernels, from about 4 large ears
3 tablespoons finely chopped Mauna Loa macadamias
1$^1/_2$ cups Mauna Loa Macadamia Oil

In a small bowl, stir together flour, baking powder, baking soda and sugar with a fork. In a medium bowl, whisk together eggs, garlic, fish sauce and red curry paste until smooth. Whisk in flour mixture until thoroughly blended. Stir in corn and macadamias and continue mixing until completely incorporated into the batter, which should be thick and smooth.

In a large skillet, heat oil over medium-high heat. Drop batter by the table-spoonful into the hot oil. Cook until deep golden brown, about 2 minutes per side. Drain on paper towels.

MAKES ABOUT 45 FRITTERS

Green Salad with Roquefort Flans and Macadamias

This is a divinely rich recipe, so I prefer to follow it with a lighter entrée like pasta or fish.

ROQUEFORT FLANS:

6 ounces Roquefort cheese, crumbled

2 eggs

1 tablespoon minced fresh Italian parsley

1/4 teaspoon salt

1/8 teaspoon freshly ground pepper

2/3 cup heavy cream

VINAIGRETTE:

1/4 cup red wine vinegar

1 small shallot, minced

1 tablespoon snipped fresh chives

1 teaspoon Dijon mustard

1/2 teaspoon salt

1/4 teaspoon freshly ground pepper

1/2 cup Mauna Loa Macadamia Oil

1 head Bibb lettuce, torn into bite-sized pieces

1/2 cup chopped Mauna Loa macadamias, lightly toasted

Preheat oven to 350 degrees F. Lightly butter six 3/4-cup ramekins.

For the Roquefort flans: Place a sieve over a bowl. Using the back of a spoon, press the Roquefort through the sieve. Whisk in the eggs, parsley, salt and pepper until smooth. Whisk in the cream. Divide mixture evenly among the ramekins. Place the ramekins in a shallow pan and add enough hot water to the pan to come halfway up the outsides of the ramekins. Bake for 20 minutes, or until flans are just set in the middle. Remove and cool completely.

For the vinaigrette: In a small bowl, whisk together vinegar, shallot, chives, Dijon, salt and pepper. Slowly add the oil in a thin stream, whisking constantly, until all oil is incorporated.

Toss the lettuce with the vinaigrette and divide onto 6 salad plates. Run a small sharp knife around the edges of the flans to loosen them. Invert onto salads. Sprinkle with macadamias.

SERVES 6

Macadamia-Crusted Monterey Jack

✺ *You may use a sweet or sourdough baguette, as you prefer. Each choice will confer it's own subtle spin on this wonderful winter starter. It makes a cozy aside for soup as well.*

1 baguette, cut into $1/2$-inch thick slices
1 large clove garlic, cut in half
$1/2$ cup all-purpose flour
1 egg, lightly beaten
1 cup finely chopped Mauna Loa macadamias
12 ounces Monterey Jack cheese, cut into about eight $1/2$-inch thick slices
3 tablespoons Mauna Loa Macadamia Oil

✺ Preheat oven to 350 degrees F.

Place baguette slices in a single layer on a baking sheet. Bake for about 15 minutes, or until lightly toasted. Remove from oven and rub the cut side of the garlic on top of the toasts. Discard garlic.

Place flour in a shallow bowl. Place egg in another shallow bowl. Place macadamias in another shallow bowl. Dredge cheese slices in flour, then dip in egg. Finally, place in macadamias, pressing to coat both sides.

In a large non-stick skillet, heat the oil over medium heat. Add the crusted cheese slices and fry about 5 minutes per side, or until nicely browned on both sides. Place 2 pieces of toast each on 8 salad plates and top with a slice of hot cheese. Serve immediately.

SERVES 8

Roasted Beet Salad with Blood Oranges and Macadamias

Blood oranges impart a very special flavor to this salad, but if they are unavailable in your area, regular oranges will do nicely.

1 pound beets, scrubbed, with tops and tails trimmed

VINAIGRETTE:
1 tablespoon sherry vinegar
1 teaspoon Dijon mustard
$1/2$ teaspoon salt
$1/4$ teaspoon freshly ground pepper
2 tablespoons Mauna Loa Macadamia Oil

2 blood oranges, peeled and all pith removed with a paring knife
4 ounces arugula, torn into bite-sized pieces
$1/4$ cup chopped Mauna Loa macadamias

Preheat oven to 400 degrees F.

Place beets on a roasting pan and roast for about 45 minutes, or until tender. Remove from oven and let cool.

For the vinaigrette: In a bowl, whisk together the sherry vinegar, Dijon mustard, salt and pepper. Whisk in the oil.

When the beets are cool enough to handle, peel and cut into $1/2$-inch cubes. Place in the bowl with the vinaigrette. Cut the blood oranges into $1/2$-inch sections and add to beets. Toss well.

Divide the arugula onto 4 plates. Divide the beet mixture on top and sprinkle with macadamias.

SERVES 4

MAIN COURSES PART II

Sea Bass, Asparagus and Macadamias with Warm Lemon Curry Vinaigrette

Alejandro Fernandez at the Outrigger Prince Kuhio Hotel in Honolulu has offset the sweetness of the sea bass by adding the tangy acidity of the lemon vinaigrette. Serve with chive-sented sticky rice for a tasteful and tasty presentation.

WARM LEMON CURRY VINAIGRETTE:

1/4 cup freshly squeezed lemon juice

1/4 cup heavy cream

3/4 teaspoon curry powder

Salt, to taste

1/2 cup extra-virgin olive oil

1 teaspoon white wine vinegar

4 (6-ounce) sea bass filets

4 tablespoons extra-virgin olive oil

Salt and freshly ground pepper, to taste

32 asparagus spears

1/3 cup extra-virgin olive oil

1 teaspoon sugar

Salt and freshly ground pepper, to taste

1/2 cup finely chopped Mauna Loa macadamias, lightly toasted

Lemon zest, for garnish

1 star fruit, for gransh

For the warm lemon curry vinaigrette: In a small saucepan, combine lemon juice, cream, curry powder and salt. Simmer over low heat until hot. Pour into a blender. With motor running, add oil in a thin, steady stream until all is incorporated. Blend in the vinegar. Return to saucepan and keep warm.

For the fish: In a large skillet, heat 4 tablespoons oil. Place sea bass filets into skillet and cook 4 to 5 minutes per side, or until fish starts to flake. Season with salt and pepper.

In a large skillet, combine asparagus, oil, sugar, salt and pepper. Sauté over medium heat for 1 minute. Add water to barely cover and cook over high heat until asparagus is just tender.

Divide asparagus spears between 4 plates and sprinkle with 2 tablespoons macadamias. Top with a sea bass filet and drizzle with the warm lemon curry vinaigrette.

SERVES 4

Pad Thai

This is one of the most famous of all Thai dishes, and the key to this rendition is using the freshest ingredients possible. Don't be afraid to go to your local Asian grocery shop and ask for help when choosing produce, spices or other ingredients that are unfamiliar.

PAD THAI SAUCE:

1/3 cup hot water

1 tablespoon dried tamarind

1/2 cup fish sauce

1/2 cup ketchup

1/3 cup chopped cilantro

1/4 cup freshly squeezed lime juice

1/4 cup sugar

1/4 cup water

1 tablespoon dried red chile flakes, or to taste

1 tablespoon paprika

12 ounces rice noodles

2 tablespoons sesame oil

6 tablespoons Mauna Loa Macadamia Oil, in all

6 cloves garlic, minced

1 onion, chopped

1 cup bean sprouts, cut in half

2 eggs, beaten

2 boneless half chicken breasts, cubed

8 ounces medium uncooked shrimp, shelled and deveined

1 cup diced extra-firm tofu

3/4 cup finely chopped Mauna Loa macadamias, for garnish

1/2 cup bean sprouts, cut in half, for garnish

6 scallions, chopped, for garnish

For the Pad Thai sauce: In a small bowl, combine hot water and tamarind. Let stand 30 minutes then strain. Reserve liquid and discard solids. In a large bowl, combine tamarind liquid with remaining sauce ingredients. Mix well and set aside.

Soak the rice noodles in cold water for 30 minutes, or until soft. Drain well and toss with sesame oil until well coated. Set aside.

In a large skillet, heat 3 tablespoons of the macadamia oil over medium-high heat. Add garlic and onion and stir-fry until onion is translucent. Add bean sprouts and stir-fry until liquid evaporates but sprouts are still crunchy. Push vegetables aside and pour in the beaten eggs. Cook until set, then slice into ribbons and lightly stir into the vegetables. Transfer cooked vegetable mixture to a bowl and set aside.

Add 2 tablespoons macadamia oil to the skillet and add chicken. Stir-fry until golden. Add shrimp and stir-fry until just pink. Push meat aside and add tofu. Stir-fry until golden. Transfer to the bowl with the cooked vegetables and set aside.

Add 1 tablespoon macadamia oil into skillet and add rice noodles. Stir-fry about 3 minutes. Add reserved Pad Thai sauce and simmer, stirring often, until sauce starts to be absorbed by the noodles. Add reserved vegetables and meat mixture and stir gently until mixture is well coated. Simmer until heated through but not soupy. Garnish with macadamias, bean sprouts and scallions.

SERVES 6 TO 8

Penne with Chanterelles and Macadamias

When it's time to impress the boss, negotiate a contract or meet your future inlaws, this fusion of old-world flavors with the new-world nuttiness of buttery macadamias is guaranteed to get you that raise, clinch that deal and win over Mom and Dad.

3 shallots, minced

1/2 cup dry vermouth

5 tablespoons butter

2 cups chanterelles, sliced

1 cup heavy cream

6 ounces Parmesan, grated

1 cup finely chopped Mauna Loa macadamias

1/4 cup sour cream

2 tablespoons minced fresh parsley

1 teaspoon salt

1/4 teaspoon white pepper

1] pound penne, cooked in boiling salted water
    until *al dente*, then drained

Chopped fresh parsley, for garnish

In a saucepan, combine shallots and vermouth. Simmer over medium heat until mixture is reduced to a syrup. Add butter and mushrooms and sauté until tender. Stir in cream and reduce by one third. Stir in Parmesan, macadamias, sour cream, parsley, salt and pepper and cook until heated through.

Toss hot pasta with sauce and sprinkle with chopped parsley. Serve immediately.

SERVES 6

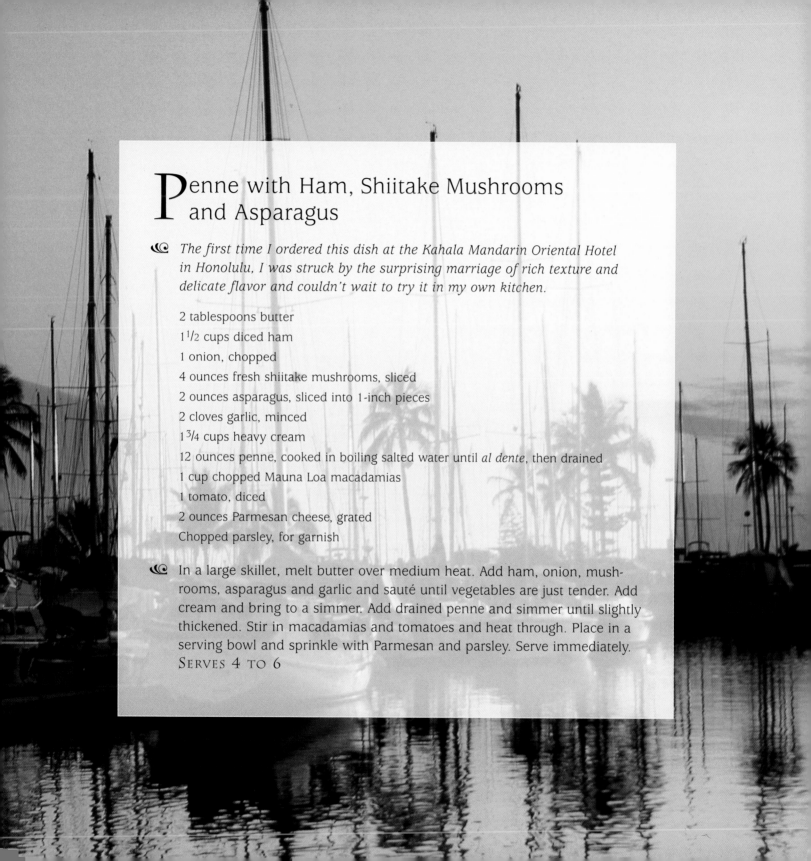

Penne with Ham, Shiitake Mushrooms and Asparagus

The first time I ordered this dish at the Kahala Mandarin Oriental Hotel in Honolulu, I was struck by the surprising marriage of rich texture and delicate flavor and couldn't wait to try it in my own kitchen.

2 tablespoons butter

1 1/2 cups diced ham

1 onion, chopped

4 ounces fresh shiitake mushrooms, sliced

2 ounces asparagus, sliced into 1-inch pieces

2 cloves garlic, minced

1 3/4 cups heavy cream

12 ounces penne, cooked in boiling salted water until *al dente*, then drained

1 cup chopped Mauna Loa macadamias

1 tomato, diced

2 ounces Parmesan cheese, grated

Chopped parsley, for garnish

In a large skillet, melt butter over medium heat. Add ham, onion, mushrooms, asparagus and garlic and sauté until vegetables are just tender. Add cream and bring to a simmer. Add drained penne and simmer until slightly thickened. Stir in macadamias and tomatoes and heat through. Place in a serving bowl and sprinkle with Parmesan and parsley. Serve immediately. Serves 4 to 6

Macadamia-Crusted Tofu with Noodles

This healthful and flavorful summer dish is a study in contrasts. The crunch of the sautéed macadamias is a surprising complement to the silky creaminess of the tofu.

1 package (about 14 ounces) extra-firm tofu, drained

1/4 cup sake

2 tablespoons soy sauce

1 teaspoon sesame oil

DRESSING:

2 tablespoons prepared black bean sauce

2 tablespoons sake

2 tablespoons sesame oil

1 tablespoon soy sauce

1 tablespoon sugar

8 ounces dried Chinese egg noodles or spaghetti

2 bunches watercress, coarsely chopped

1 bunch scallions, thinly sliced

1/4 cup finely ground Mauna Loa macadamias

2 tablespoons Mauna Loa Macadamia Oil

Slice tofu crosswise into 8 pieces. Drain on paper towels. In a shallow dish, stir together sake, soy sauce and sesame oil. Place tofu in dish, cover and marinate in the refrigerator for 2 hours. Remove tofu from marinade and drain briefly. Reserve excess marinade.

For the dressing: In a large bowl, whisk together all dressing ingredients until smooth. Add reserved marinade.

Cook noodles in boiling water until *al dente*, then drain. Place hot noodles in dressing and toss to coat. Add watercress and scallions and toss.

Place ground macadamias on a plate. Dip tofu into macadamias and press lightly to coat one side. In a large skillet, heat macadamia oil over medium heat. Cook tofu, macadamia crust side down, for about 3 minutes or until golden brown. Turn and cook on the other side until golden brown.

To serve, divide noodles between 4 plates and place 2 pieces of tofu, macadamia side up, on top of each.

SERVES 4

Stir-Fried Chicken and Vegetables with Macadamia Pesto over Linguini

Worlds collide in the most delicious way imaginable thanks to William Kaluakini Trask of the Illikai Yacht Club. A Far Eastern stir-fry meets Western European pasta resulting in a felicitous detente of flavors.

1/4 cup finely chopped Mauna Loa macadamias

1 tablespoon minced fresh ginger

1 clove garlic, minced

1 tablespoon minced fresh cilantro

1/4 cup Mauna Loa Macadamia Oil, in all

6 boneless half chicken breasts, sliced across the grain 1/2-inch thick

1/4 pound daikon, peeled and sliced into 1/4-inch matchsticks

2 carrots, peeled and sliced diagonally into 1/4-inch ovals

1 red bell pepper, seeded and sliced into 1/4-inch rings

1 onion, peeled and sliced into 1/4-inch half-moons

4 ounces snow peas

Salt and freshly ground pepper, to taste

16 ounces linguini, cooked in boiling salted water until *al dente* and drained

4 scallions, sliced into 1-inch pieces, for garnish

In the bowl of a food processor, combine macadamias, ginger, garlic, cilantro and 2 tablespoons macadamia oil and process until smooth. Set aside.

In a wok, heat the remaining macadamia oil over high heat, add half of the pesto and the chicken. Stir-fry the chicken until brown, then remove with a slotted spoon and set aside. Add the daikon, carrots and red pepper to the wok and stir-fry the vegetables for 1 minute. Then add the onion and snow peas and stir-fry until the vegetables are cooked, but still firm.

Add the remaining pesto along with the reserved chicken. Mix well, and stir-fry until the chicken is cooked through. Season with salt and pepper. Serve over the linguini and garnish with scallions.

SERVES 6

Crab Cakes

This is a lovely light luncheon dish when served with a green salad or makes a hearty supper when joined by a cup of clam chowder, roasted herbed potatoes, and some zesty cole slaw.

1/4 cup mayonnaise

1 egg

1 tablespoon freshly squeezed lemon juice

1 teaspoon dry mustard

1/2 teaspoon salt

1/2 teaspoon Tabasco sauce

1/2 teaspoon Worcestershire sauce

1/4 teaspoon white pepper

1 pound crab meat

1/2 cup fresh bread crumbs

1/2 cup finely chopped Mauna Loa macadamias

1 small onion, finely minced

1 stalk celery, finely minced

About 3 cups fresh bread crumbs for coating crab cakes

4 tablespoons butter

4 tablespoons Mauna Loa Macadamia Oil

In a large bowl, combine mayonnaise, egg, lemon juice, dry mustard, salt, Tabasco sauce, Worcestershire sauce and white pepper and whisk until well blended. Stir in crab, 1/2 cup bread crumbs, macadamias, onion and celery until mixed. Do not overmix. Form mixture into 8 patties. Coat crab cakes with additional bread crumbs. Place on baking sheet and chill for 30 minutes to make handling easier.

In a large skillet, heat butter and oil together over medium heat. Cook the crab cakes for about 4 minutes per side until nicely browned. Remove and keep warm.

SERVES 4

Macadamia-Breaded Chicken with Guava Lime Sauce

If guavas are scarce where you live, you may substitute with mangoes, which are generally easier to find. The tangy sauce is a delightful partner for the rich, hearty chicken and a delightful reminder of your last trip to the islands.

GUAVA LIME SAUCE:

3/4 cup guava purée

1/4 cup dry white wine

Juice from 1 lime

3/4 cup heavy cream

1 cup cold butter, cut into small pieces

Salt and freshly ground pepper, to taste

MACADAMIA BREADED CHICKEN:

2 1/2 cups all-purpose flour, in all

2 cups water

2 cups panko bread crumbs

1/2 cup finely chopped Mauna Loa macadamias

6 boneless half chicken breasts, skin removed

Salt and freshly ground pepper, to taste

1/4 cup Mauna Loa Macadamia Oil

For the guava lime sauce: In a medium saucepan, whisk together the guava purée, white wine and lime juice. Simmer over medium heat until reduced by half, stirring often. Add the cream and reduce by half again. Reduce the heat to low and, whisking constantly, add the butter a little at a time. As soon as all the butter is incorporated, remove from heat and season with the salt and pepper. Strain through a fine sieve. Serve warm.

For the macadamia breaded chicken: Place 1/2 cup of the flour in a shallow dish. In a second shallow dish, blend together the remaining 2 cups flour and the water until smooth. In a third shallow dish, mix the panko and the macadamias.

Season the chicken breasts with salt and pepper. Lightly dust with flour, dip the breasts into the batter, and then in the panko mixture, coating thoroughly. Cover and chill until ready to cook.

In a large heavy skillet, heat the oil over medium-high heat. Sauté chicken breasts until golden brown and crispy on both sides, about 4 minutes per side.

Ladle the sauce onto the serving plate and place the hot chicken breasts on top.

SERVES 6

Traditionally macadamia nuts are gathered by hand after falling naturally from the tree, although some growers now use mechanical sweepers and collecters. The cost of harvesting the nuts is exceedingly high since the pickers must return many times to the orchards to gather the fresh fallen nuts. Additionally, since the the nuts don't ripen all at once, the harvest stretches for seven months.

Macadamia and Crab-Filled Onaga

The chefs at the Kea Lani Hotel on Maui created this rich recipe, sparkling with the spunky addition of pickled ginger in the filling.

MACADAMIA AND CRAB FILLING:

8 ounces crab meat

1 cup finely chopped Mauna Loa macadamias, lightly toasted

$1/4$ cup finely chopped scallions

2 tablespoons finely chopped pickled ginger

2 tablespoons sesame seeds, lightly toasted

2 tablespoons freshly squeezed lemon juice

1 egg, lightly beaten

1 teaspoon salt

$1/2$ teaspoon white pepper

6 (4-ounce) onaga filets (red snapper) about $3/4$-inch thick

$1/4$ cup Mauna Loa Macadamia Oil

For the macadamia and crab filling: In a large bowl, combine all filling ingredients and mix well.

Lay the onaga filet, flat side down, on a cutting board. Using a sharp knife, cut a pocket lengthwise in each filet. Stuff pocket with one sixth of the filling mixture. Secure pocket with toothpicks. Repeat with remaining filets.

In a large skillet, heat 2 tablespoons of the oil over high heat. Add 3 stuffed filets and cook for about 3 minutes per side. Remove cooked filets and keep warm. Add remaining 2 tablespoons oil to skillet and cook remaining filets. Serve immediately.

SERVES 6

Spicy Macadamia Noodles

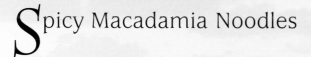 *This is a piquant pasta that I love to slurp up by the fire on cold, rainy, Northern California nights.*

3/4 cup chopped Mauna Loa macadamias, lightly toasted
1/4 cup lightly packed cilantro leaves
3 scallions, chopped
3 tablespoons sugar
2 tablespoons rice vinegar
1 tablespoon sesame oil
1 teaspoon chopped garlic
1 teaspoon chopped fresh ginger
1/2 teaspoon sambal oelek
1/4 cup soy sauce
8 ounces spaghetti, cooked in boiling water until *al dente* then drained

In the bowl of a food processor, combine macadamias, cilantro, scallions, sugar, rice vinegar, sesame oil, garlic, ginger and sambal oelek and process until smooth. With motor running, add soy sauce and process until thoroughly combined. Pour mixture into a large serving bowl. Add the hot spaghetti and toss well. Serve immediately.

SERVES 4 TO 6

Chicken Ding with Macadamias

Eileen Yin-Fei Lo, author of From the Earth: Chinese Vegetarian Cooking *and* The Chinese Way: Healthy Low-Fat Cooking from China's Regions, *has generously shared this special variation on an Oriental classic. The Chinese name for this dish is Gung Bo Gai Ding which translates as Small Squares for the Crown Prince.*

1 cup chicken stock
$1/2$-inch long piece fresh ginger, peeled and lightly crushed
8 ounces boneless chicken breasts, cut into $1/2$-inch cubes

SAUCE:
2 tablespoons of reserved chicken stock
$1^1/2$ tablespoons oyster sauce
2 teaspoons tapioca starch or cornstarch
$1^1/2$ teaspoons light soy sauce
$1/4$ teaspoon sesame oil
$1/8$ teaspoon white pepper

1 tablespoon Mauna Loa Macadamia Oil
$1^1/2$ teaspoons minced garlic
1 teaspoon minced fresh ginger
1 tablespoon hoisin sauce
1 tablespoon Shao-Hsing wine or dry sherry
4 ounces snow peas, cut into $1/2$-inch pieces
$1/2$ cup bamboo shoots, cut into $1/2$-inch pieces
$1/3$ cup water chestnuts, cut into $1/4$-inch pieces
2 tablespoons of reserved chicken stock
$1/2$ cup chopped Mauna Loa macadamias

In a saucepan, combine 1 cup chicken stock and crushed ginger. Bring to a boil over high heat. Blanch the chicken for 1 1/2 minutes, or until it turns white. Remove from heat, strain chicken and set aside. Reserve stock. Discard ginger.

For the sauce: In a small bowl, combine all sauce ingredients and whisk until smooth. Set aside.

Heat wok or large skillet over high heat for 30 seconds. Add macadamia oil and swirl to coat wok. When a wisp of white smoke appears, add garlic and ginger and stir-fry briefly. Add hoisin sauce and stir to mix. Add reserved chicken and stir to coat. Add wine and stir-fry briefly. Stir in snow peas then bamboo shoots and water chestnuts. Add 2 tablespoons reserved chicken stock and stir-fry for 2 minutes. Make a well in the center of the mixture, stir reserved sauce, pour into the well and stir-fry to mix thoroughly. When sauce darkens and thickens, remove from heat and transfer to a warmed serving dish. Sprinkle with macadamias.

SERVES 4

The macadamia is a beautiful evergreen tree which grows to a height of about 40 feet. It takes four to seven years for the tree to bear fruit and it will yield a crop for up to 150 years. In fact, Haiwaiian trees first planted in the nineteenth century are still alive and bearing!

Fried Red Snapper with Pandanus Beurre Blanc and Breadfruit Relish

This tropical show-stopper from Stephen Marquard at the Outrigger Marshall Island resort is well worth the effort. Don't be afraid of the exotic ingredients— you can substitute papaya purée for the pandanus, and steamed sweet potato for the breadfruit in this beautiful Micronesian dish.

BREADFRUIT AND ORANGE RELISH:

1 ripe breadfruit *or* sweet potato, steamed

2 cups oranges, peeled and diced

1/3 cup chopped scallions, green part only

1/3 cup chopped red onion

2 tablespoons olive oil

2 tablespoons Mauna Loa Macadamia Oil

Salt and freshly ground pepper, to taste

FRIED RED SNAPPER:

1 cup all-purpose flour

6 eggs, beaten

2 cups freshly grated coconut

2 cups finely chopped Mauna Loa macadamias

1 cup panko bread crumbs

4 (6-ounce) red snapper filets

Salt and freshly ground pepper, to taste

1/2 cup clarified butter

PANDANUS BEURRE BLANC:

2 cups dry white wine

1 cup rice vinegar

1 cup freshly squeezed orange juice

1/3 cup chopped shallots

2 tablespoons peppercorns

3 sprigs fresh thyme

1 1/4 cups pandanus *or* papaya purée

1/2 cup heavy cream

1 cup cold butter, cut into small pieces

Salt and freshly ground white pepper, to taste

For the breadfruit and orange relish: Peel, core and slice breadfruit (or peel and slice sweet potato). Steam until tender. When cool enough to handle, dice and place in a large bowl. Add diced oranges, scallions, red onions, olive oil and macadamia oil. Stir gently to mix. Season to taste with salt and white pepper. Cover and chill for 1 hour to let flavors blend.

For the pandanus beurre blanc: In a heavy saucepan, combine wine, vinegar, orange juice, shallots, peppercorns and thyme. Bring to a boil, then reduce heat to medium and simmer until mixture has reduced to about 1 cup. Add pandanus (or papaya) purée and cream and simmer for about 4 minutes, or until slightly thickened. Strain mixture, discard solids and return to sauce-pan. Heat pandanus mixture over low heat and add butter, a little at a time, whisking well to incorporate after each addition. Place sauce in the top of a double boiler over warm, not simmering, water. Do not let sauce get too warm or it will separate.

For the fried red snapper: Put flour in a shallow dish. Put eggs in a separate shallow dish. Stir together coconut, macadamias and panko in a third shallow dish. Season red snapper filets with salt and pepper. Dredge in flour, shaking off any excess. Dip filets in eggs, letting excess drip off. Place in macadamia mixture, pressing coating firmly onto both sides.

In a large skillet, heat clarified butter over medium-high heat. Add filets and saute until just cooked through and well browned on both sides. Drain on paper towels and keep warm.

To serve, divide pandanus beurre blanc onto 4 plates. Place fish in the center of plates and spoon breadfruit and orange relish over the top.

SERVES 4

Vietnamese Cellophane Noodle Salad with Grilled Shrimp

I have a particular soft spot in my heart for this salad because I first enjoyed it at a little Vietnamese restaurant in Paris while attending cooking school at the Hotel Ritz—one of the happiest times in my life.

DRESSING:

¹/₃ cup Mauna Loa Macadamia Oil

¹/₄ cup rice vinegar

¹/₄ cup chopped cilantro

3 tablespoons fish sauce

1 tablespoon freshly sqeezed lime juice

1 tablespoon sesame oil

1 tablespoon sugar

1 large shallot, minced

1¹/₂ teaspoons minced fresh mint

1 teaspoon minced garlic

1 or 2 fresh Thai chiles (or other small
   hot chiles), minced

¹/₄ teaspoon white pepper

CELLOPHANE NOODLE SALAD:

4 cups water

5 ounces cellophane noodles
   (also called saifun)

4 ounces fresh spinach, washed and
   chopped

2 tomatoes, diced

1 mango, peeled and diced

1 small red onion, thinly sliced

1 small red pepper, thinly sliced

¹/₂ cup chopped Mauna Loa macadamias,
   lightly toasted

1 pound large uncooked shrimp, peeled
   with tails left on

Mauna Loa Macadamia Oil

For the dressing: In a large serving bowl, whisk together all dressing ingredients and set aside.

For the cellophane noodle salad: In a saucepan, bring water to a rolling boil. Add cellophane noodles, remove from heat, and set aside until softened, about 20 minutes. Drain well. Add to dressing and stir. Add spinach, tomatoes, mango, red onion, red pepper and macadamias and toss well.

Prepare grill. Brush shrimp with oil and grill until pink. Add to noodles and toss well. Serve at room temperature or chilled.

SERVES 6 TO 8

Macadamia-Crusted Onaga with Hawaiian Pesto

Chef Laurent Poulain from the Ritz-Carlton Mauna Lani on the Big Island has combined Pacific Rim, Polynesian and Italian cuisines to achieve exciting new flavor combinations and to keep Hawaii at the culinary crossroads of the world.

HAWAIIAN PESTO:

1 cup packed cilantro leaves

1/2 cup chopped Mauna Loa macadamias

3 ounces Parmesan cheese, grated

6 scallions, chopped

2 tablespoons chopped fresh ginger

2 tablespoons freshly squeezed lemon juice

1 clove garlic, chopped

1 teaspoon sesame oil

1/2 teaspoon salt

1/2 cup Mauna Loa Macadamia Oil

4 (6-ounce) onaga filets (red snapper)

Salt and freshly ground pepper, to taste

1/2 cup all-purpose flour

2 eggs, beaten

1 cup finely chopped Mauna Loa macadamias

3 tablespoons Mauna Loa Macadamia Oil

For the Hawaiian pesto: In the bowl of a food processor, combine cilantro, macadamias, Parmesan, scallions, ginger, lemon juice, garlic, sesame oil, and salt. Process until smooth. With motor running, add oil in a thin stream until all is incorporated. Set aside.

Season filets with salt and pepper. Dredge filets in flour then dip in egg. Press macadamias onto each side. In a large skillet, heat oil over medium-high heat. Add the crusted filets and cook for about 2 minutes per side. Keep warm until all filets are cooked. Drizzle with Hawaiian pesto and serve immediately.

SERVES 4

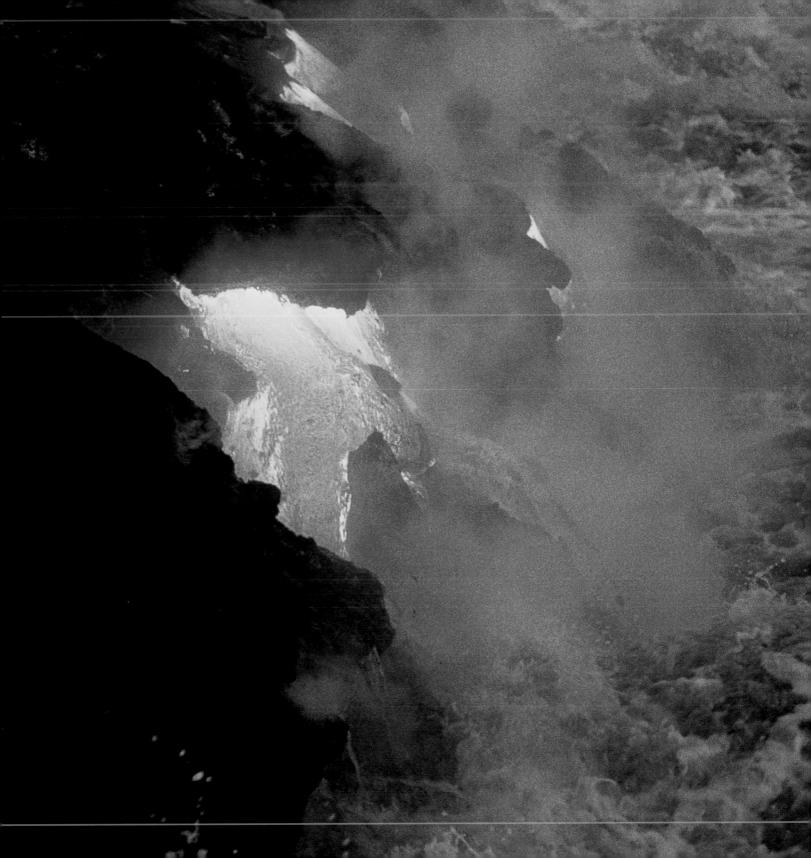

Rum-Baked Fish with Hot Mango Salsa

I like my salsa hot, so be prepared—this is a 5-alarm, Caribbean-inspired, firework display of flavors! Just reduce the amount of the chile to adjust the heat.

Hot Mango Salsa:

2 ripe mangoes, peeled and diced

1 red bell pepper, seeded and diced

1/2 cup chopped Mauna Loa macadamias, lightly toasted

1 Habanero chile, seeded and minced

3 tablespoons cider vinegar

1/2 teaspoon salt

2 tablespoons peppercorns

10 whole allspice berries

10 whole cloves

1 cup dark rum

1 cup soy sauce

3/4 cup sugar

6 (6-ounce) Chilean sea bass filets

Preheat oven to 425 degrees F.

For the hot mango salsa: In a medium bowl, combine all ingredients and mix well. Let stand 30 minutes before serving to allow flavors to blend.

In a medium saucepan, toast the peppercorns, allspice and cloves over medium-high heat, just until spices start to pop. Then place spices in a mortar and pestle and crush. Return spices to saucepan and add rum, soy sauce and sugar. Reduce heat to medium and simmer until mixture is reduced by half. Take care that rum does not ignite, cover with a lid if it does.

Strain mixture and discard the spices. Place the fish filets in a baking pan and pour the strained liquid over them. Marinate 10 minutes. Turn fish and place in oven. Bake for about 10 minutes, or until fish is cooked through. Serve with hot mango salsa.

SERVES 6

Singha Thai's Stir-Fried Chicken with Macadamias

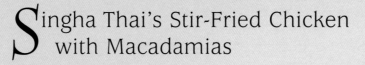 *Chef Chai Chaowasaree at Singha Thai Cuisine in Honolulu shares a simple, flavorful dish that's perfect for occasions when you want to spend less time in the kitchen and more time with your guests.*

2 tablespoons Mauna Loa Macadamia Oil

4 boneless chicken breasts, thinly sliced

1 zucchini, peeled and cut into matchsticks

1 small onion, thinly sliced

2 small dried hot chiles, or to taste

^{1}/4 cup oyster sauce

2 tablespoons fish sauce

^{1}/3 cup water

1 cup chopped Mauna Loa macadamias

4 scallions, thinly sliced

Freshly ground pepper, to taste

In a large skillet, heat oil over high heat. Add chicken and stir-fry until just cooked through. Add zucchini, onion, chiles, oyster sauce and fish sauce and stir-fry 1 minute. Add water and stir-fry 2 minutes. Add macadamias, scallions and pepper and stir-fry 2 minutes. Serve over plain white rice.

SERVES 4

Shrimp in Coconut, Banana and Macadamia Sauce

This dish is unapologetically rich, so just count your blessings rather than calories and enjoy!

2 tablespoons Mauna Loa Macadamia Oil
1 large banana, peeled and halved lengthwise
6 shallots, chopped
2 cloves garlic, minced
2 cups unsweetened coconut milk
1 cup chopped Mauna Loa macadamias
Juice of 2 limes
2 tablespoons fish sauce
Salt and freshly ground pepper, to taste
1 pound medium shrimp, shelled and deveined
Chopped fresh cilantro, for garnish

In a sauté pan, heat 1 tablespoon of the oil over medium heat. Add the banana halves and sauté until golden on both sides. Put banana in a blender. Add the shallots and garlic to the pan and sauté just until fragrant. Place shallots and garlic in a blender. Add the coconut milk, macadamias, lime juice, and fish sauce to the blender. Blend until smooth.

Pour sauce into a saucepan and bring to a boil. Reduce heat to medium and simmer until reduced by one third and slightly thickened, about 10 minutes, stirring frequently.

Add remaining 1 tablespoon oil to sauté pan and heat over high heat. Add shrimp and sauté until shrimp turn pink, about 1 or 2 minutes.

Add shrimp to sauce and simmer for 2 or 3 minutes to heat through. Serve over plain rice and sprinkle with cilantro.

SERVES 4.

Trout Stuffed with Crab and Macadamias

The delicacy of the trout is the perfect foil for the richness of the crab. Wild rice makes the perfect accompaniment.

^{1}/$_3$ cup basmati rice

^{1}/$_4$ teaspoon salt

4 tablespoons butter, in all

^{2}/$_3$ cup finely chopped Mauna Loa macadamias

4 shallots, minced

3 ounces oyster mushrooms, chopped

8 ounces fresh Dungeness crab meat

1 teaspoon freshly squeezed lemon juice

Salt and freshly ground pepper, to taste

6 whole trout, cleaned and rinsed

Flour

3 tablespoons Mauna Loa Macadamia Oil

Lemon slices, for garnish

Snipped fresh chives, for garnish

Place the rice in a sieve and rinse under cold running water until water runs clear. Let drain. In a small saucepan, add the rice with ^{2}/$_3$ cup water, ^{1}/$_4$ teaspoon salt and 1 teaspoon butter. Bring to a boil stirring occasionally. Reduce heat to low, cover and simmer gently for 20 minutes. Remove from heat and let stand for five minutes.

In a sauté pan, melt 1 tablespoon butter over medium heat. Add the macadamias and lightly sauté until just golden brown. Remove macadamias and set aside. Melt remaining 2^1/$_2$ tablespoons butter and sauté the shallots and mushrooms for 1 minute. Mix in the rice, crab, lemon juice and macadamias and season with the salt and pepper. Sauté until mixture is heated through, about 3 minutes. Remove from heat.

Stuff the cavities of the trout with the crab filling and secure with a thin skewer. Dredge trout lightly in flour. In a large skillet, heat the macadamia oil over medium heat. Add the trout and sauté about five minutes per side, or until golden brown and cooked through.

Place fish on a warm serving platter. Garnish with lemon slices and chives and serve immediately.

SERVES 6

Macadamia-Crusted Rack of Lamb

I adore lamb and rack of lamb is especially popular around holiday time. This is the simplest, never-fail recipe imaginable that is a godsend during, what for most of us, is the most hectic time of the year.

1/2 cup finely chopped Mauna Loa macadamias
1/3 cup lightly packed fresh Italian parsley leaves
1 tablespoon Dijon mustard
3 cloves garlic
1 teaspoon salt
1/2 teaspoon freshly ground pepper
1 rack of lamb with 8 ribs

Preheat oven to 400 degrees F.

Place macadamias, parsley, Dijon, garlic, salt and pepper in the bowl of a food processor and process until almost smooth. Set aside.

Lightly score the fat side of the rack of lamb. Cover rib tips with foil. Place fat side up on a broiling pan. Roast for 20 minutes. Remove from oven and pat macadamia mixture on top of the lamb. Return to oven and continue to roast an additional 10 to 15 minutes, or until internal temperature reaches 140 degrees F. Remove from oven and let lamb rest for 10 minutes before carving.

SERVES 4

Ricotta and Mashed Potato Ravioli with Sundried Tomato and Macadamia Pesto

The combination of potato and ricotta gives this ravioli a robust texture that's tempered by the rich tanginess of the pesto.

RICOTTA AND MASHED POTATO FILLING:

1 cup cold mashed potatoes

1 cup ricotta cheese

1 ounce ($1/4$ cup) freshly grated Parmesan cheese

2 egg yolks

1 tablespoon minced shallot

2 cloves garlic, minced

1 teaspoon minced fresh chives

1 teaspoon minced fresh Italian parsley

1 teaspoon salt

$1/4$ teaspoon white pepper

SUNDRIED TOMATO AND MACADAMIA PESTO:

3 ounces ($3/4$ cup) freshly grated Parmesan cheese

$1/2$ cup sundried tomatoes in oil, drained

$1/4$ cup finely chopped Mauna Loa macadamias

1 tablespoon minced fresh basil

2 cloves garlic, minced

$1/2$ teaspoon salt

$1/4$ cup olive oil

1 egg

1 teaspoon water

1 (12-ounce) package wonton wrappers

For the ricotta and mashed potato filling: In a large bowl, combine potatoes, ricotta, Parmesan, egg yolks, shallot, garlic, chives, parsley, salt and white pepper. Beat until smooth. Cover with plastic wrap and set aside in the refrigerator.

For the sundried tomato and macadamia pesto: In the bowl of a food processor, combine Parmesan, tomatoes, macadamias, basil, garlic and salt and process until smooth. With the motor running, add the oil in a thin stream until all oil is incorporated. Set aside.

To assemble the raviolis: In a small bowl, whisk together egg and water until smooth. Place a wonton wrapper on a lightly floured surface and, using a pastry brush, brush lightly with the egg mixture. Place about 2 teaspoons of filling on the center of wrapper and place a second wrapper on top, pressing sides together to seal. Place on a baking sheet. Repeat until all the filling is used.

Bring a large pot of salted water to a rolling boil. Add half of the raviolis at a time, return to a boil and cook until *al dente.* Remove cooked raviolis with a slotted spoon. Repeat with remaining raviolis. Divide between 6 plates and spoon pesto over the top.

SERVES 6

Persian Pomegranate Chicken

I adapted this heady Persian recipe from one given to me by my dear friend Ghassem Farzanah. You'll probably need to venture out to a Middle Eastern grocery store for the pomegranate molasses, but it will be worth the effort— I promise.

1 tablespoon Mauna Loa Macadamia Oil
1 onion, chopped
1 pound boneless chicken thighs, cut into 1-inch cubes
2 cups finely chopped Mauna Loa macadamias
2/3 cup pomegranate molasses
2/3 cup water
1/2 teaspoon salt
1/2 teaspoon freshly ground pepper

In a heavy pot, heat the oil over medium heat. Add the onions and sauté until translucent. Stir in the chicken, macadamias, pomegranate molasses, water, salt and pepper and bring to a boil. Reduce heat to low, cover and simmer about 1 to 1 1/2 hours, stirring often, or until chicken is tender and mixture is very thick. Serve over rice pilaf.

SERVES 6

Mussaman Beef Curry

I discovered this fragrant curry on a trip to the southern, mostly Muslim, part of Thailand. Mussamen curry paste can be found at your local Asian grocery.

1/3 cup hot water

1 tablespoon dried tamarind

3 tablespoons Mauna Loa Macadamia Oil

1 1/2 pounds round steak or stewing beef, cut into 1-inch cubes

1 tablespoon mussaman curry paste

1 onion, chopped

3 cups unsweetened coconut milk

2 tablespoons fish sauce

1 tablespoon sugar

1/2 teaspoon cardamom

1 large potato, peeled and cut into 1/2-inch cubes

1/2 cup chopped Mauna Loa macadamias

In a small bowl, combine hot water and tamarind. Let stand 30 minutes then strain. Reserve liquid and discard solids. Set aside.

In a large pot, heat oil over medium-high heat. Add beef and brown well on all sides. Add curry paste and stir to coat beef thoroughly. Add onion and stir to mix. Stir in coconut milk, reserved tamarind liquid, fish sauce, sugar and cardamom and bring to a boil. Reduce heat to low, cover and simmer 1 to 1 1/2 hours, stirring often, until beef is very tender. Add potato and macadamias, cover and simmer an additional 30 minutes, stirring often, or until potato is tender.

Serve over steamed rice.

SERVES 6 TO 8

ℬREADS

Macadamia and Currant Scones

Macadamias transform an English tea time classic into a South Pacific specialty.

2 1/2 cups all-purpose flour
4 1/2 teaspoons baking powder
1 teaspoon salt
2/3 cup sugar
1/2 cup cold butter, cut into small pieces
1/2 cup finely chopped Mauna Loa macadamias
1/2 cup currants
1/2 cup heavy cream
3 eggs, in all
2 teaspoons milk

Preheat oven to 350 degrees F. Lightly butter two baking sheets.

In a large bowl, sift together the flour, baking powder and salt. Stir in the sugar. Cut in the butter until the mixture resembles coarse meal. Stir in the macadamias and currants. Make a well in the center. In a separate bowl, blend the cream with 2 eggs until smooth. Pour cream mixture into the well in the flour mixture. Stir until mixture holds together. Gather dough into a ball, it will be moist. Divide in half and flatten into discs.

Turn dough out onto a lightly floured board and roll out to a 1-inch thickness. Cut out rounds using a 3-inch cookie cutter. Transfer to prepared baking sheets. Blend remaining egg and milk together and brush tops of scones with mixture. Bake for about 20 minutes or until golden brown.

MAKES 12 SCONES

Hawaiian Granola

My husband and I discovered California on this stuff and I guarantee that it's the tastiest granola you'll ever try at any elevation. It has sustained us from the hills of San Francisco to the High Sierra, from Death Valley to Heavenly Valley, and from Disneyland to the Donner Pass.

5 cups oatmeal

2 cups sweetened flaked coconut

2 cups chopped Mauna Loa macadamias

2 cups dried bananas

3/4 cup butter

1/4 cup honey

1/4 cup packed brown sugar

1 cup chopped dried pineapple

Preheat oven to 350 degrees F. Lightly oil two jelly roll pans.

In a large bowl, combine oatmeal, coconut and macadamias. Place bananas in the bowl of a food processor and pulse until coarsely chopped. Stir bananas into oatmeal mixture. In a medium saucepan, whisk together the butter, honey and brown sugar over medium heat until smooth. Pour the butter mixture over the oatmeal mixture and stir until evenly moistened.

Divide the mixture between the prepared pans and bake for 10 minutes. Remove pans from oven and stir well. Return pans to oven and bake an additional 10 minutes, or until golden brown. Let the granola cool, then return to large bowl. Stir in the pineapple. Cool completely and store in an airtight container.

MAKES ABOUT 14 CUPS

Macadamia Dinner Rolls

Light and fluffy with the nutty and buttery flavor of macadamias, these are a staple at Merriman's Restaurant in Kamuela on the Big Island.

1 1/4 cups warm water

1 package active dry yeast

1 teaspoon sugar

2 tablespoons Mauna Loa Macadamia Oil

2 teaspoons salt

1/2 cup whole wheat flour

1/2 cup finely chopped Mauna Loa macadamias, lightly toasted

3 to 3 1/2 cups bread flour

In a large bowl, stir together warm water, yeast and sugar. Let stand until foamy. Stir in oil and salt. Stir in whole wheat flour and macadamias until smooth. Stir in 2 1/2 cups of the bread flour until all is absorbed. Slowly beat in enough of the remaining bread flour to form a stiff dough. Turn dough out onto a lightly floured surface and knead until dough is smooth and satiny, about 10 minutes. Place dough in a lightly oiled bowl and turn to coat. Cover and let rise until doubled in size, about 1 1/2 hours.

Punch dough down and knead a few times on a lightly floured surface. Cut into 12 equal pieces and shape into balls. Place on a baking sheet and dust lightly with flour. Slash tops with a razor blade or a very sharp knife. Let rise uncovered for 30 minutes.

Preheat oven to 375 degrees F.

Bake rolls for 10 to 15 minutes, or until golden brown.

MAKES 12 ROLLS

Macadamia Bread

Honolulu's Kahala Mandarin Oriental Hotel serves this delicious quick bread as the perfect accompaniment to a cup of Earl Grey tea. Try it toasted with unsalted butter and a sharp marmalade or under a generous dollop of softened cream cheese. It freezes well so you can always keep a loaf on hand.

1 cup plus 2 tablespoons sugar

$3/4$ cup butter, softened

3 eggs

$1^1/2$ teaspoons vanilla extract

$3/4$ teaspoon almond extract

$2^1/2$ cups all-purpose flour

1 teaspoon baking powder

$1/4$ teaspoon salt

$2/3$ cup heavy cream

$1^1/2$ cups chopped Mauna Loa macadamias

Preheat oven to 325 degrees F. Butter and flour two 8 x 4-inch loaf pans.

In a large bowl, cream together sugar and butter. Beat in eggs, vanilla and almond extract until light and fluffy. Sift flour, baking powder and salt together into a small bowl. Add flour mixture to butter mixture alternately with cream, beating well after each addition. Stir in macadamias. Divide batter into prepared pans and bake for 35 to 40 minutes, or until toothpick inserted in the center comes out clean. Cool in pans.

MAKES 2 LOAVES

Banana Macadamia Muffins

These moist, cake-like muffins are favorites at the Kahala Mandarin Oriental Hotel in Honolulu. They will be right at home on your breakfast table, too.

1 cup (2 bananas) mashed bananas
1 1/3 cups cake flour
1 cup sugar
1/2 cup bread flour
1 1/4 teaspoons baking soda
2 eggs
1/4 cup Mauna Loa Macadamia Oil
1/2 cup buttermilk
1 cup finely chopped Mauna Loa macadamias

Preheat oven to 350 degrees F. Lightly oil a muffin tin.

In a large bowl, combine bananas, cake flour, sugar, bread flour and baking soda and beat until smooth. Add eggs and beat until smooth. Add macadamia oil and beat until smooth. Add buttermilk and beat until smooth. Stir in macadamias.

Pour batter into muffin tins almost filling them. Bake for about 20 minutes, or until a toothpick inserted in the center of a muffin comes out clean.

MAKES ABOUT 18 MUFFINS

Chocolate and Cream Cheese-Stuffed Macadamia Braid

The Mauna Loa Macadamia Recipe Contest is held annually on the Big Island during the Hilo Harvest Moon Festival. Not surprisingly, Heather Crockett was one of the winners with this spectacular Easter centerpiece.

DOUGH:

1 package active dry yeast

1/4 cup warm water

1/4 cup melted butter

1/4 cup warm milk

1/4 cup sugar

1 egg

1 teaspoon salt

3 cups all-purpose flour

FILLING:

8 ounces cream cheese

1/2 cup sugar

1 teaspoon vanilla extract

1 cup semisweet chocolate chips

1 cup chopped Mauna Loa macadamias

GLAZE:

1 cup powdered sugar

2 tablespoons strong brewed coffee

1/4 cup finely chopped Mauna Loa macadamias

For the dough: In a large bowl, stir together yeast and warm water until dissolved. Stir in butter, milk, sugar, egg and salt until smooth. Stir in flour until you have a soft dough. Turn out onto a lightly floured surface and knead until dough is smooth and satiny, about 10 minutes. Place dough in a lightly oiled bowl and turn to coat. Cover and let rise until doubled in size, about 1 1/2 hours.

For the filling: In a large bowl, beat together cream cheese, sugar and vanilla until smooth. Stir in chocolate chips and macadamias.

Punch down dough and turn out onto a lightly floured surface. Roll out into a 15 x 10-inch rectangle. Place dough on a baking sheet. With a sharp knife, lightly mark the dough lengthwise into thirds. Spread the filling down the middle third of the dough. With the sharp knife, make diagonal 1-inch wide cuts down the left and right sides of the dough. Starting from the top, overlap the 1-inch pieces of dough alternately across the filling until you have what looks like a braid. Let rise uncovered for 30 minutes.

Continued on next page.

For the glaze: In a small bowl, whisk together powdered sugar and coffee until smooth.

Preheat oven to 350 degrees F. Bake braid for 25 to 30 minutes, or until golden brown. Remove from oven. Brush the glaze over the top of the braid with a pastry brush and sprinkle with macadamias. Serve warm.

Sweet Potato and Macadamia Muffins

My husband Richard surprised me one evening with these chewy muffins comprised of two favorite Hawaiian flavors.

$2/3$ cup sugar
$1/3$ cup butter, softened
1 egg
1 teaspoon vanilla extract
$1^3/4$ cups all-purpose flour
$1^1/2$ teaspoons baking powder
$1/2$ teaspoon salt
$2/3$ cup milk
$1^1/2$ cups lightly packed finely grated sweet potato
$1/2$ cup chopped Mauna Loa macadamias

Preheat oven to 375 degrees F. Lightly oil a 3-inch muffin tin.

In a large bowl, cream sugar and butter together until light and fluffy. Beat in egg and vanilla until smooth. In a separate bowl, stir flour, baking powder and salt together with a fork. Add to sugar mixture alternately with milk, beating until just combined. Fold in sweet potato and macadamias.

Pour batter into muffin tins almost filling them. Bake for about 25 minutes, or until a toothpick inserted in the center comes out clean. Serve warm.

MAKES ABOUT 12 MUFFINS

Buttermilk and Macadamia Pancakes

These are the lightest, loftiest pancakes in the world from the best cook in the world, Marcia Whipple, my Mom.

6 eggs, separated
1 teaspoon baking soda
1 2/3 cups buttermilk
1 1/2 cups all-purpose flour
1 teaspoon baking powder
1/2 teaspoon salt
1/4 cup butter, melted and cooled
1 tablespoon sugar
1/2 cup finely chopped Mauna Loa macadamias
Butter
Pure maple syrup

In a large bowl, lightly beat egg yolks. In a separate bowl, dissolve baking soda in buttermilk and then stir into egg yolks. Sift together flour, baking powder and salt. Gently fold into egg mixture just enough to moisten ingredients. Gently fold in melted butter and set aside. Beat egg whites until soft peaks form. Add sugar and continue beating until stiff. Fold egg whites gently into batter and stir in macadamias. Batter should be lumpy.

Heat a griddle to 350 degrees F. Grease griddle lightly with butter and pour about 1/4 cup of batter per pancake. Cook until a few bubbles break on top and bottom is golden brown. Turn the pancakes and cook until golden brown.

Serve hot with butter and maple syrup.

SERVES 4

Macadamia Sticky Buns

Although this recipe requires some time and attention, I find this series of steps takes me into a kind of baking meditation. And the rewards are both spiritual and tangible. Be sure to make them a day ahead.

DOUGH:

1/4 cup warm water

1 package active dry yeast

1/2 cup milk, scalded

1/4 cup melted butter

1/4 cup sugar

2 eggs

1 teaspoon salt

3 cups bread flour

TOPPING:

1 cup packed brown sugar

1/4 cup butter

2 tablespoons light corn syrup

1 cup chopped Mauna Loa macadamias

FILLING:

2 tablespoons melted butter

2 tablespoons packed brown sugar

2 teaspoons cinnamon

1/2 cup raisins

Oil a 10-inch pie plate.

For the topping: In a small saucepan, combine brown sugar, butter and corn syrup. Simmer over medium heat until sugar dissolves, stirring often. Pour syrup into pie plate and sprinkle macadamias evenly over the syrup. Set aside.

For the dough: Place the warm water in a small bowl and sprinkle in the yeast. Stir and let stand for 10 minutes to dissolve. In a large mixing bowl, combine the scalded milk and butter and let cool to lukewarm. Stir in the sugar, eggs, salt and yeast mixture. Stir in the flour and beat vigorously to make a soft dough. Turn out dough onto a lightly floured surface and knead until smooth and satiny, about 10 minutes. Roll out into an 18 x 10-inch rectangle.

For the filling: Spread the melted butter over the dough to within 1/2-inch of the edges. In a small bowl, stir together the brown sugar and cinnamon with a fork. Evenly sprinkle brown sugar mixture and raisins over the dough.

Starting from the long side, roll up dough as you would for a jelly roll. Pinch the seam together to seal. Cut roll crosswise with a serrated knife into

Continued on next page.

12 pieces about 1¹/2-inches thick. Place rolls, cut side up, on the syrup mixture. Cover tightly with plastic wrap and refrigerate for 2 to 24 hours.

Preheat oven to 375 degrees F.

Remove buns from refrigerator, uncover, and let stand for 10 minutes at room temperature. Place on a baking sheet to catch any drips and bake for 30 to 40 minutes, or until a toothpick inserted in the center of the buns comes out clean and buns are golden brown. Let the pan cool on a rack for 5 minutes then invert onto a serving plate. Serve warm.

MAKES 12 STICKY BUNS

Although the macadamia nut has become virtually synonomous with Hawaii, Australia is also a major source for this most delectable nut. Other countries and places where the macadamia is grown include southern California, Costa Rica, Brazil, Guatemala, South Africa, Kenya, Malawi and Zimbabwe.

ꙮCOOKIES

Macadamia Coconut Icebox Cookies

In addition to the great flavor marriage of macadamias and coconut, these cookies are ideal to keep as dough in the freezer and need only a few minutes to bake — thanks to Bev Kype at Merriman's Restaurant on the Big Island.

1^1/$_2$ cups butter, softened
1^1/$_4$ cups sugar
1 tablespoon vanilla extract
2 cups all-purpose flour
1 teaspoon baking soda
^{1}/$_4$ teaspoon salt
2 cups oatmeal
2 cups chopped Mauna Loa macadamias
1 cup sweetened flaked coconut

In a large bowl, cream butter and sugar together until fluffy. Beat in vanilla. Sift together flour, baking soda and salt and add to butter mixture. Beat until smooth. Add oatmeal, macadamias and coconut and beat until well blended. Divide dough into 3 portions. Place each portion on a piece of plastic wrap and form into a log about 10 inches long. Wrap and freeze for at least 2 hours, and up to 2 months.

Preheat oven to 325 degrees F. Line baking sheets with parchment paper.

Remove frozen dough and let stand at room temperature for 5 minutes. Slice each log crosswise into 24 rounds. Place on prepared baking sheets about 1 inch apart. Bake for 12 to 15 minutes or until golden brown.

MAKES 72 COOKIES

Chocolate Macadamia Shortbread Cookies

Mauna Loa Macadamia Recipe Contest winner Becky Speere has contributed an outstanding chocolate cookie with a delicate shortbread crust blanketed in a rich, chocolate topping.

SHORTBREAD CRUST:

2 cups butter, softened

1 cup sugar

1 teaspoon vanilla extract

1/2 teaspoon salt

4 cups all-purpose flour

CHOCOLATE MACADAMIA FILLING:

2 cups semisweet chocolate chips

1/4 cup butter

6 eggs

1 cup raw sugar

2/3 cup light corn syrup

2 teaspoons vanilla extract

2 cups finely chopped Mauna Loa
    macadamias, lightly toasted

Preheat oven to 375 degrees F.

For the shortbread crust: In a large bowl, cream together the butter, sugar, vanilla and salt until light and fluffy. Beat in the flour until you have a crumbly dough. Press mixture evenly into the bottom of an 18 x 12-inch jelly roll pan. Bake for about 15 minutes, or until lightly golden.

For the chocolate macadamia filling: In the top of a double-boiler, melt together chocolate and butter over simmering water. Whisk until smooth. Set aside.

In a large bowl, beat the eggs and raw sugar together until well blended. Stir in chocolate mixture, corn syrup and vanilla until smooth. Stir in the macadamias. Pour mixture over the shortbread crust. Bake an additional 25 to 30 minutes, or until filling has set. Remove from oven and cool completely. Cut into 2-inch squares.

MAKES 54 COOKIES

Chocolate-Topped Mocha Cookies

I have always loved the sophistication that the flavor of coffee lends to just about everything, but especially to chocolate.

1/2 cup butter, softened

3/4 cup sugar

1/4 cup packed brown sugar

1 egg

1 tablespoon instant coffee

2 teaspoons vanilla extract

1 1/2 cups all-purpose flour

1 teaspoon baking powder

1/2 teaspoon salt

1 cup finely chopped Mauna Loa macadamias

1/2 cup semisweet chocolate chips

1 teaspoon vegetable shortening

Preheat oven to 350 degrees F.

In a large bowl, cream butter, sugar and brown sugar together until smooth. Add egg, instant coffee and vanilla and beat until light and fluffy. Add flour, baking powder and salt and beat until smooth. Stir in macadamias. Shape into 1-inch balls and place on baking sheets. Bake for 15 minutes, or until golden brown. Cool on racks.

In the top of a double boiler, melt chocolate chips and shortening together over simmering water. Stir until smooth. Remove from heat and spread a dollop of chocolate on top of each cookie.

MAKES 36 COOKIES

Orange and Macadamia Biscotti

These biscotti, from Italian chef and caterer Patricia Caringella, have a wonderful texture and a bright orange flavor. They are pure heaven dipped in a mug of steaming hot cocoa.

1 cup sugar

$1/2$ cup butter, softened

2 eggs

1 tablespoon vanilla extract

1 teaspoon almond extract

2 teaspoons freshly squeezed orange juice

2 teaspoons minced orange zest

$2^1/3$ cups all-purpose flour

$1^1/2$ teaspoons baking powder

$1/8$ teaspoon salt

1 cup finely chopped Mauna Loa macadamias

Preheat oven to 375 degrees F.

In a large bowl, cream sugar and butter together until light and fluffy. Add eggs, vanilla, almond extract, orange juice and orange zest and beat until smooth. Add flour, baking powder and salt and beat until smooth. Stir in macadamias. Divide dough into 4 portions. Lightly flour your hands because the dough will be sticky, and shape into logs. Place 3 inches apart on a baking sheet. Bake for 15 to 20 minutes, or until light golden brown. Remove from oven and slice crosswise about $1/2$-inch thick. Place slices, cut side up, on baking sheets and return to oven. Bake an additional 15 to 20 minutes, or until crisp and dry. Cool on a rack.

MAKES ABOUT 3 DOZEN BISCOTTI

Honey Date Macadamia Bars

The flavors of honey and dates have a natural affinity which is further enhanced by the toasty texture of macadamias.

2 eggs
1/2 cup honey
2 tablespoons melted butter
3/4 cup all-purpose flour
1/2 teaspoon baking powder
1/4 teaspoon salt
1/2 cup chopped dates
1/2 cup finely chopped Mauna Loa macadamias
Powdered sugar

Preheat oven to 350 degrees F. Lightly oil an 8 x 8-inch baking pan.

In a large bowl, beat eggs until frothy. Add the honey and butter and beat until smooth. Add the flour, baking powder and salt and beat until smooth. Stir in dates and macadamias. Pour batter into prepared pan and bake for 25 minutes, or until a toothpick inserted in the center comes out clean. While warm, cut into squares and dust with powdered sugar.

MAKES 16 BARS

Mauna Loa® Macadamia Brittle

This is the original Mauna Loa Macadamia brittle recipe and is one of their most popular mail-order products.

1^1/$_2$ cups sugar

^{1}/$_2$ cup packed brown sugar

^{2}/$_3$ cup light corn syrup

^{1}/$_4$ cup water

^{1}/$_4$ cup butter

^{1}/$_2$ teaspoon salt

1 cup chopped Mauna Loa macadamias

1 teaspoon baking soda

^{1}/$_2$ teaspoon vanilla extract

Lightly oil a baking sheet.

In a heavy saucepan, combine sugar, brown sugar, corn syrup and water. Cook over medium-high heat, stirring constantly, until a candy thermometer placed in the syrup near the center of the pan reads 260 degrees F. Add butter and salt and continue to cook until the temperature reaches 295 degrees F. Remove from heat and stir in the macadamias, baking soda and vanilla.

Pour the brittle onto prepared baking sheet and spread to a ^{1}/$_4$-inch thickness using a rubber spatula. Cool completely at room temperature. Break into pieces and store in an airtight container.

MAKES ABOUT 1^1/$_4$ POUNDS OF BRITTLE

Chocolate Macadamia Biscotti

This is another great biscotti recipe, this time from Elaine Harai, another Mauna Loa Macadamia Recipe Contest winner. I like to offer my guests several different types of biscotti, and since they keep so well, they are easy to prepare in advance and keep on hand.

2 cups all-purpose flour
$1/3$ cup unsweetened cocoa powder
$1 1/2$ teaspoons baking powder
$1/2$ teaspoon salt
$1 1/4$ cups sugar
$1/2$ cup butter, softened
2 eggs
$1 1/2$ teaspoons vanilla extract
1 cup finely chopped Mauna Loa macadamias
$2/3$ cup semisweet chocolate chips

Preheat oven to 350 degrees F.

In a small bowl, sift together flour, cocoa powder, baking powder and salt. In a large bowl, cream sugar and butter together. Beat in eggs and vanilla. Gradually beat in flour mixture until all is incorporated. Stir in macadamias and chocolate chips.

Turn dough out onto a lightly floured surface and knead until smooth. Divide dough in half and form into logs about 10 inches long. Place 3 inches apart on a baking sheet and bake for 25 to 30 minutes, or until toothpick inserted in the center comes out clean. Let cool for 10 minutes.

Cut logs into $1/2$-inch slices and place, cut side up, on baking sheets. Bake for an additional 15 minutes, or until lightly browned. Turn over and bake an additional 15 minutes, or until lightly browned. Cool completely on a rack.

MAKES ABOUT 3 DOZEN BISCOTTI

Chocolate Macadamia Fudge

The secret to making a creamy fudge is the final vigorous beating which prevents sugar crystals from forming. The contrast of the creamy white macadamias in the dark fudge makes this confection pleasing to the eye as well as to the palate.

2 cups sugar

1 cup evaporated milk

2 tablespoons corn syrup

$1/2$ teaspoon salt

2 ounces unsweetened chocolate

2 tablespoons butter

1 teaspoon vanilla extract

1 cup chopped Mauna Loa macadamias

Lightly oil an 8 x 8-inch pan.

In a heavy saucepan, stir together sugar, evaporated milk, corn syrup and salt. Add chocolate and simmer over medium heat, stirring often, until chocolate melts. Raise heat to high and cook, stirring often, until candy thermometer reaches 238 degrees F. Remove from heat and stir in butter. Let mixture cool to lukewarm. Add vanilla and beat vigorously until mixture loses its gloss. Stir in macadamias and spread into prepared pan. Cut into squares when cool.

MAKES ABOUT $1\frac{1}{4}$ POUNDS OF FUDGE

Macadamia Biscotti

Fred Halpert at the Brava Terrace in St. Helena, California, twice-baked these biscotti for extra crunch. Dip them in a cup of Kona coffee for a light breakfast, serve them with a pot of Earl Grey for a mid-afternoon tea or offer them with your favorite liqueur after a casual, late-night supper.

1/2 cup butter, softened

1 cup packed brown sugar

1/3 cup sugar

1 teaspoon vanilla extract

3/4 teaspoon finely minced orange zest

1 egg

1 1/2 cups all-purpose flour

2/3 cup ground almonds

1 teaspoon baking powder

1/2 teaspoon cinnamon

1/4 teaspoon salt

1 cup finely chopped Mauna Loa macadamias

In a large bowl, cream together butter, brown sugar, sugar, vanilla and orange zest. Add egg and beat until smooth. Add flour, ground almonds, baking powder, cinnamon and salt and blend until smooth. Stir in macadamias.

Divide the dough in half and roll into 12-inch cylinders. Cover with plastic and refrigerate for at least 3 hours.

Preheat oven to 325 degrees F. Line two baking sheets with parchment paper.

Remove dough and discard plastic wrap. Place dough at least 3 inches apart on prepared baking sheet. Bake for 35 minutes or until golden and dry to the touch. Remove from oven and allow to cool slightly.

Cut the logs diagonally into $^3/4$-inch slices. Arrange the biscotti, cut side up, on the baking sheets so that they do not touch each other. Return to oven and bake an additional 25 minutes, or until crisp and dry. Cool on racks.

MAKES 2 DOZEN BISCOTTI

Macadamia Butter Nuts

These delightful tea cakes are easy for children to make and a must on a holiday cookie platter.

1 cup butter, softened
1 cup powdered sugar, sifted
1 teaspoon vanilla extract
$2^1/2$ cups all-purpose flour
$^1/4$ teaspoon salt
1 cup finely chopped Mauna Loa macadamias
Powdered sugar

Preheat oven to 400 degrees F.

In a large bowl, cream together butter and sugar. Beat in vanilla. Beat in flour and salt until smooth. Stir in macadamias. Shape dough into $1^1/2$-inch balls. Place on baking sheets and bake for about 9 minutes, or until just beginning to color. Remove from oven and, while still warm, roll in powdered sugar. Place on waxed paper to cool. Store in an airtight container.

MAKES ABOUT 48 COOKIES

Double Mac Cookies

If you are a peanut butter cookie fan, wait until you taste this macadamia version from Mauna Loa Macadamia Recipe Contest winner Koi Lee.

2 cups Mauna Loa macadamias
1/4 cup butter, softened
1/2 cup packed brown sugar
1/2 cup sugar
1 egg
1/2 teaspoon baking powder
1/2 teaspoon salt
1/2 teaspoon vanilla extract
1 1/2 cups sifted all-purpose flour
3/4 cup finely chopped Mauna Loa macadamias

Preheat oven to 375 degrees F. Lightly oil a baking sheet.

Place 2 cups macadamias in the bowl of a food processor. Process until smooth and creamy. Set aside.

In a large bowl, beat butter, brown sugar and sugar together until creamy. Add reserved macadamia butter, egg, baking powder, salt and vanilla and beat until smooth. Add flour and beat until well blended. Stir in the 3/4 cup macadamias.

Using about 1 tablespoon of dough at a time, roll into 1-inch balls and place on prepared baking sheet. Press the tops down lightly with a fork. Bake for about 10 to 15 minutes, or until golden brown.

MAKES ABOUT 30 COOKIES

Macadamia and Coffee Chocolate Bars

I think the best advice for the novice cook is this: A recipe will only be as good as the ingredients you make it with, so always use the best that you can afford. I think Ghiradelli chocolate is some of the best available.

1 cup butter, softened
1 cup sugar
1 egg
$1/4$ cup coffee-flavored liqueur
$1^3/4$ cups all-purpose flour
6 ounces Ghirardelli Bittersweet Chocolate, broken into 1-inch pieces
$3/4$ cup finely chopped Mauna Loa macadamias

Preheat oven to 350 degrees F. Grease a 15 x 10-inch jelly roll pan.

In a large bowl, cream the butter and sugar together until fluffy. Add the egg and liqueur, and mix well. Gradually mix in the flour. Press the dough evenly into prepared pan. Bake 25 minutes, or until golden brown. Immediately top with chocolate and allow to melt. Spread melted chocolate evenly. Sprinkle with macadamias. Place pan on a wire rack and let cool to room temperature. Chill 10 minutes, or until chocolate has set. Store loosely covered.

MAKES ABOUT 32 BARS

Macadamia Cheesecake Brownie

Like an elite athlete in an extreme sport, I think of myself as an elite brownie recipe developer and extreme brownie baker. This is the most decadent of all the brownie recipes I have tried. If you can top it—please write to me!

BROWNIE:

8 ounces semisweet chocolate

6 tablespoons butter

4 eggs

1 1/2 cups sugar

1 cup all-purpose flour

1 teaspoon baking powder

1/2 teaspoon salt

1 1/2 cups finely chopped Mauna Loa macadamias

Powdered sugar

CHEESE TOPPING:

8 ounces cream cheese

1/2 cup sugar

1/4 cup butter, softened

1 egg

1/2 teaspoon vanilla extract

Preheat oven to 350 degrees F. Lightly oil a 9-inch springform pan.

For the brownies: In the top of a double boiler, melt together chocolate and butter over simmering water. Remove from heat and let cool. In a large bowl, beat the eggs until foamy. Gradually beat in the sugar until light and fluffy. Stir in the chocolate mixture until blended. Stir in the flour, baking powder and salt until smooth. Stir in macadamias. Spread batter evenly into prepared pan.

For the cheese topping: In a large bowl, beat cream cheese and sugar together until smooth, scraping the sides often. Beat in butter until fluffy. Gradually beat in egg and vanilla.

Spoon cheese topping over chocolate batter. Swirl together lightly to marble. Bake for 60 to 75 minutes, or until center is just set. Cool on a rack then cover and chill. Sprinkle with powdered sugar.

SERVES 12

Macadamia Meringue Cookies

Lighter-than-air and easier-than-pie, meringue is one those things that looks much more difficult to make than it really is. If you've never attempted it before, try these simple cookies and achieve instant success.

3 egg whites
1/8 teaspoon salt
1 cup sugar
2 cups finely chopped Mauna Loa macadamias

Preheat oven to 325 degrees F. Butter and flour two baking sheets.

In a large bowl, beat egg whites and salt until foamy. Continue beating until soft peaks form. Gradually add sugar and continue beating until stiff and glossy. Fold in macadamias. Drop by the heaping teaspoonful onto prepared baking sheets. Bake for 15 to 20 minutes, or until lightly browned. Cool on racks.

MAKES ABOUT 48 COOKIES

White Chocolate and Fudge Marbled Brownies

These gorgeous, gooey brownies, dense with macadamias and swirls of fudge, came from the kitchen of Mauna Loa Macadamia Recipe Contest winner Miriam Baroga.

FUDGE FILLING:

1 cup semisweet chocolate chips

1/4 cup butter

1/4 cup half-and-half

1 egg

1 teaspoon vanilla extract

WHITE CHOCOLATE BROWNIE:

1 1/2 cups white chocolate chips

1/2 cup butter

1/2 cup sugar

2 eggs

1/4 cup half-and-half

1 teaspoon vanilla extract

1/4 teaspoon salt

1 1/4 cups all-purpose flour

1 cup chopped Mauna Loa macadamias

Preheat oven to 325 degrees F. Lightly butter an 8 x 8-inch baking pan.

For the fudge filling: In the top of a double boiler, combine the semi-sweet chocolate chips and butter and melt over simmering water. Whisk until smooth, then remove from heat and allow to cool. In a large bowl, beat the half-and-half, egg and vanilla together until smooth. Beat in the chocolate mixture until well blended. Set aside.

For the white chocolate brownie: In the top of a double boiler, combine the white chocolate chips and butter and melt over simmering water. Whisk until smooth, then remove from heat and allow to cool. In a large bowl, beat the sugar and eggs together until pale and fluffy. Beat in the half-and-half, vanilla and salt until smooth. Beat in the flour until well blended. Beat in the white chocolate mixture and half of the macadamias.

Pour two thirds of this mixture into prepared pan. Spread the fudge filling over, then spoon on remaining brownie mixture. Using a knife, gently swirl the batters together until it looks marbled. Sprinkle remaining macadamias over the top. Bake for about 45 minutes, or until a toothpick inserted in the center comes out clean. Cool in the pan then cut into squares.

MAKES 9 BARS

The macadamia tree was first discovered in Australia in 1843, by the Prussian emigre and botanical explorer, Friedrich Wilhelm Ludwig Leichardt. The nut was later named for the renowned chemist and Australian parlamentarian Dr. John Macadam.

Melt-in-Your-Mouth Macadamia Shortbread Cookies

 *Daphne Higa at the Grand Wailea Resort on Maui, aptly named her deceptively light, notoriously rich shortbread cookies.*

2 cups butter, softened
1 cup plus 2 tablespoons sugar
1 teaspoon vanilla extract
1/2 teaspoon salt
3 cups plus 3 tablespoons all-purpose flour
1 cup cake flour
1 3/4 cups finely chopped Mauna Loa macadamias
1/4 cup raw sugar

Preheat oven to 350 degrees. Lightly oil two baking sheets.

In a large bowl, cream butter, sugar, vanilla and salt together until light and fluffy. Add flour and cake flour and beat until smooth.

In a shallow dish, stir together macadamias and raw sugar. Form dough into 1-inch balls and roll in macadamia mixture. Place 2-inches apart on prepared baking sheets, and flatten slightly. Bake for about 15 minutes, or until golden brown. Cool on rack.

MAKES ABOUT 56 COOKIES

Macadamia Rum Bars

Macadamias join forces with sweet coconut and spicy rum to conjure up the heady romance of the tropics.

CRUST:
1/2 cup butter, softened
1/4 cup sugar
1 cup all-purpose flour

ICING:
1 1/4 cups powdered sugar, sifted
2 tablespoons butter, softened
1 tablespoon milk
1 teaspoon dark rum
1/2 teaspoon vanilla extract

FILLING:
1 1/4 cups packed brown sugar
2 eggs
2 tablespoons all-purpose flour
1 tablespoon dark rum
1 teaspoon vanilla extract
1/2 teaspoon salt
1/4 teaspoon baking powder
1 cup sweetened flaked coconut
1 cup finely chopped Mauna Loa macadamias

Preheat oven to 350 degrees F. Lightly oil a 13 x 9-inch baking pan.

For the crust: In a large bowl, cream butter and sugar together until fluffy. Beat in the flour until well blended. Press dough into the bottom of prepared pan. Bake for 15 to 20 minutes or until lightly browned.

For the filling: In a large bowl, beat the brown sugar and eggs together. Beat in the flour, rum, vanilla, salt and baking powder until smooth. Beat in coconut and macadamias. Spread mixture evenly over crust. Bake an additional 20 minutes, or until golden brown. Remove from oven and cool completely.

For the icing: In a bowl, whisk together powdered sugar, butter, milk, rum and vanilla until smooth. Spread icing over cooled filling. Cut into 2-inch squares.

MAKES ABOUT 36 BARS

Millionaire's Shortbread

Not just for the rich and famous, Mauna Loa Macadamia Recipe Contest winner Kay Cabrera insists that you don't have to be a millionaire, just feel like one while you enjoy her incomparable cookies.

SHORTBREAD:
2 cups all-purpose flour

1/2 cup powdered sugar

1/4 teaspoon baking powder

1 cup cold butter, cut into small pieces

1/2 teaspoon vanilla extract

FILLING:
2 1/2 cups sugar

1/2 cup water

3/4 cup heavy cream

3/4 cup plus 2 tablespoons butter, cut into pieces

2 cups chopped Mauna Loa macadamias, toasted

GLAZE:
8 ounces bittersweet chocolate, chopped

3/4 cup heavy cream

6 tablespoons butter

1/4 cup light corn syrup

Preheat oven to 350 degrees F. Lightly oil a 13 x 9-inch baking pan.

For the shortbread: In a medium bowl, sift together flour, powdered sugar and baking powder. Cut in the butter and vanilla until mixture holds together. Press dough evenly into the bottom of the prepared pan. Bake for about 20 minutes, or until the edges are lightly browned and shortbread appears dry and crisp. Remove from oven and cool.

For the filling: In a heavy saucepan, stir together the sugar and water. Bring to a boil over high heat until the sugar begins to caramelize. Swirl the pan gently to allow the syrup to caramelize evenly. When caramel is deep brown, add the cream all at once; stand back since it will sputter and boil up. Remove from heat and swirl pan until the boiling subsides and mixture is evenly blended. Put butter on top of the caramel, letting it melt. Stir until well blended, then stir in the macadamias. Spread filling evenly over short-bread crust. Bake an additional 15 to 20 minutes, or until caramel begins to bubble in the center. Remove from oven and cool completely.

For the glaze: Place the chopped chocolate in a bowl. In a small saucepan, combine the cream, butter and corn syrup and bring to a boil over medium-high heat. Pour cream mixture over chocolate and whisk gently until smooth. Pour glaze onto caramel and tip pan to spread evenly. Cool completely. To serve, cut into 2-inch squares.

MAKES ABOUT 36 COOKIES

*Each macadamia nut tree can
produce about 100 pounds of
in-shell macadamia nuts per year.
After shelling, only about 20 pounds
of creamy white kernels remain.*

Triple-Chocolate Macadamia Icebox Cookies

These are the ultimate in drop-dead decadent chocolate cookies. Make the dough in advance to satisfy the chocolate urge whenever it strikes. This is a great way to get your kids in the kitchen after school and start them baking!

1 cup semisweet chocolate chips
2 ounces unsweetened chocolate
2 tablespoons butter
$3/4$ cup sugar
2 eggs
1 teaspoon vanilla extract
$1/3$ cup all-purpose flour
$1/4$ teaspoon baking powder
$1/8$ teaspoon salt
2 cups finely chopped Mauna Loa macadamias
$1/2$ cup white chocolate chips

In the top of a double boiler, melt together semisweet chocolate chips, unsweetened chocolate and butter over simmering water. Stir to blend well. Set aside to cool.

In a large bowl, beat together the sugar, eggs, and vanilla until mixture is pale and thick. Beat in cooled chocolate mixture until smooth. Add flour, baking powder, and salt. Beat until well blended. Stir in macadamias and white chocolate chips. The dough will be very soft and sticky. With a rubber spatula, spread dough into a log about 15 inches long onto a piece of plastic wrap. Roll up tightly, then securely wrap in another piece of plastic wrap. Freeze at least 3 hours and up to 2 months.

Preheat oven to 350 degrees F. Lightly oil two baking sheets.

Remove dough from freezer. Slice dough into $3/4$-inch thick slices and place cut side up on prepared baking sheets. Bake for about 12 minutes, or until cookies are set. Cool on baking sheets.

MAKES ABOUT 24 COOKIES

White Chip Macadamia Bars

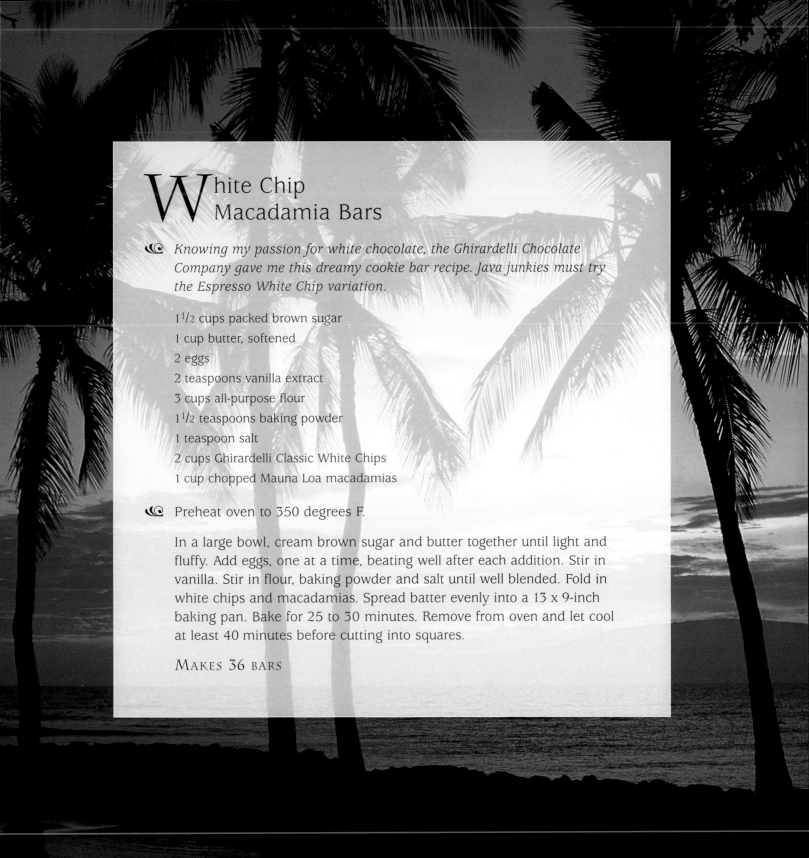

Knowing my passion for white chocolate, the Ghirardelli Chocolate Company gave me this dreamy cookie bar recipe. Java junkies must try the Espresso White Chip variation.

1^1/$_2$ cups packed brown sugar

1 cup butter, softened

2 eggs

2 teaspoons vanilla extract

3 cups all-purpose flour

1^1/$_2$ teaspoons baking powder

1 teaspoon salt

2 cups Ghirardelli Classic White Chips

1 cup chopped Mauna Loa macadamias

Preheat oven to 350 degrees F.

In a large bowl, cream brown sugar and butter together until light and fluffy. Add eggs, one at a time, beating well after each addition. Stir in vanilla. Stir in flour, baking powder and salt until well blended. Fold in white chips and macadamias. Spread batter evenly into a 13 x 9-inch baking pan. Bake for 25 to 30 minutes. Remove from oven and let cool at least 40 minutes before cutting into squares.

MAKES 36 BARS

VARIATIONS ON WHITE CHIP MACADAMIA BARS:

1. Add chocolate layer in the middle of the squares. Melt 4 ounces Ghirardelli Bittersweet Chocolate in top of a double boiler over simmering water. Prepare recipe as above, spread half of the batter in the pan. Spread melted bittersweet chocolate over batter in pan, then cover melted chocolate with remaining batter. Bake as directed.

2. *To Make Espresso White Chip Macadamia Bars:* Add $1/4$ cup brewed espresso and 1 teaspoon instant espresso powder to the batter after combining eggs. Or substitute $1/4$ cup water and 4 teaspoons instant coffee, if espresso is not available. Bake as directed.

Tropical White Chocolate and Macadamia Truffles

Merriman's Restaurant in Kamuela on the Big Island promises that the key to these truffles is to select a white chocolate specifically made for melting and dipping, and you will be assured of success with every batch.

14 ounces white chocolate, chopped
$1/2$ cup heavy cream
$1/2$ cup finely diced Mauna Loa macadamias, lightly toasted
$1/4$ cup sweetened flaked coconut, lightly toasted
Juice and finely minced zest of 2 limes

1 pound white chocolate
2 cups sweetened flaked coconut, lightly toasted

Place 14 ounces white chocolate in a bowl. In a small saucepan, bring cream to a boil. Pour over chocolate and whisk until melted. Stir in macadamias, $1/4$ cup coconut, lime juice and lime zest. Chill until firm.

Spoon chilled mixture into 24 balls of equal size. Roll in your palms to make smooth and round. Place on a plate and chill until firm.

In the top of a doubleboiler, melt remaining 1 pound white chocolate over simmering water. Using 2 forks, dip chilled truffles into melted chocolate. Shake excess chocolate back into pan and place truffle in coconut. Roll around to cover truffle and place on a plate. Repeat with all truffles. Chill until firm. Truffles can be stored in the freezer for up to 1 month.

MAKES 24 TO 26 TRUFFLES

Macadamia Toffee

A layer of chocolate dusted with macadamias covers this crunchy toffee and makes a pretty holiday gift, ready for wrapping.

1 cup butter
1 cup sugar
2 tablespoons water
1 tablespoon light corn syrup
1/2 cup chopped Mauna Loa macadamias
1/3 cup semisweet chocolate chips
1/2 cup finely chopped Mauna Loa macadamias

Lightly oil a baking sheet.

In a heavy saucepan, combine butter, sugar, water and corn syrup. Cook over high heat, stirring constantly, until candy thermometer reaches 280 degrees F. Remove from heat and stir in chopped macadamias.

Pour onto prepared baking sheet and spread thinly. Let cool about 10 minutes then sprinkle chocolate chips over the top. When the chocolate has softened, spread evenly over toffee and sprinkle with the finely chopped macadamias. When completely cool, break into pieces.

MAKES ABOUT 1½ POUNDS OF TOFFEE

ᛤDESSERTS

Cherry and Macadamia Clafoutis

Always best when cherries are at their peak, this country French dessert gets a tropical colonial twist with the addition of macadamias.

4 eggs
1 cup sugar
$1/2$ cup heavy cream
$1/2$ cup milk
1 teaspoon vanilla extract
$1/4$ teaspoon almond extract
$1/4$ cup all-purpose flour
$1/4$ cup melted butter
3 cups pitted cherries
$1/2$ cup chopped Mauna Loa macadamias

Preheat oven to 325 degrees F. Generously butter a 10-inch pie plate.

In a large bowl, beat eggs until frothy. Add sugar and beat until pale in color. Stir in cream, milk, vanilla and almond extract. Beat in flour until smooth. Beat in butter until smooth.

Pour half of the batter into prepared pie plate. Place cherries evenly over batter. Top with remaining batter. Sprinkle macadamias over the top. Bake for about 1 hour, or until golden brown.

SERVES 10

Macadamia Baklava

Chef Edward Frady of Edwards at Kanaloa on the Big Island created a tropical variation on a familiar Middle Eastern theme. This is a very, very sweet dessert.

2 cups finely chopped Mauna Loa
    macadamias
1/2 cup sugar
2 tablespoons orange flower water
2 teaspoons cinnamon
1 pound filo dough
1 cup melted butter

SYRUP:

2 cups honey
1 cup frozen orange juice
    concentrate, thawed
1 cup water
1 teaspoon freshly squeezed
    lemon juice

Preheat oven to 300 degrees F. Brush a 13 x 9-inch baking pan liberally with butter.

In a large bowl, combine macadamias, sugar, orange flower water and cinnamon and mix well. Set aside.

Unfold the filo sheets. Use only one sheet at a time and keep the remaining sheets covered with a damp tea towel to prevent them from drying out. Lay sheet evenly into prepared pan. Using a pastry brush, brush the filo with melted butter. Continue layering and buttering until you have used 15 sheets of filo. Spread macadamia mixture evenly over the dough. Cover with a sheet of filo and brush with melted butter. Continue layering and buttering until you have used 12 sheets. Using a sharp knife, cut 2-inch wide strips diagonally across the pan. Cut intersecting 2-inch wide strips to form a diamond pattern. Be sure to cut completely through baklava. Bake for 1 1/2 hours. Check during the last 20 minutes to make sure the baklava is browning, increase oven temperature to 325 degrees F if necessary.

For the syrup: In a saucepan, whisk together honey, orange juice, water and lemon juice. Bring to a boil, remove from heat and cool, then chill.

When baklava is golden brown, remove from oven and pour the cold syrup over the hot baklava. Let stand several hours to completely absorb syrup before serving.

MAKES ABOUT 60 PIECES

Juicy Apple Crisp

This old-time favorite becomes a brand new classic with the addition of macadamias. Serve with vanilla ice cream or whipped cream.

1/4 cup sugar
1 tablespoon all-purpose flour
1/2 teaspoon cinnamon
2 pounds Granny Smith apples, peeled, cored and thinly sliced

TOPPING:
1/4 cup packed brown sugar
5 tablespoons all-purpose flour
1 teaspoon cinnamon
1/4 teaspoon nutmeg
6 tablespoons cold butter
3/4 cup oatmeal
1/2 cup finely chopped Mauna Loa macadamias

Preheat oven to 350 degrees F. Generously butter a 9 x 9-inch baking pan.

In a large bowl, combine sugar, flour and cinnamon. Stir with a fork until blended. Add apples and toss to coat. Pour into prepared pan.

For the topping: In a bowl, stir together brown sugar, flour, cinnamon and nutmeg. Cut in the butter just until crumbly. Stir in the oatmeal and macadamias. Spread topping over the apples, making sure that edges are covered. Bake 40 to 45 minutes, or until apples are tender.

SERVES 6

Lime Cheesecake with Macadamia Gingersnap Crust

Somehow this cheesecake manages to be both rich and refreshing at the same time. I serve it after a spicy Asian meal like a fiery hot curry.

CRUST:

1 1/2 cups (6 ounces) gingersnap crumbs

1/2 cup finely chopped Mauna Loa macadamias

1/4 cup packed brown sugar

1/3 cup melted butter

FILLING:

1 1/2 pounds cream cheese

1 cup sugar

4 eggs

6 tablespoons freshly squeezed lime juice

2 teaspoons finely minced lime zest

Preheat oven to 350 degrees F.

For the crust: Place the gingersnap crumbs, macadamias and brown sugar in the bowl of a food processor. Pulse a few times to mix ingredients. Add the melted butter and pulse to blend. Press the mixture into the bottom of a 10-inch springform pan.

For the filling: In a large bowl, beat the cream cheese and sugar together until smooth, scraping the sides often. Add the eggs, one at a time, beating well after each addition. Add the lime juice and zest and beat until smooth.

Pour batter into the prepared crust and place springform pan on a baking sheet. Bake for about 45 minutes, or until cheesecake is very lightly golden and begins to pull away from the sides of the pan. Cool to room temperature, then cover and chill overnight.

SERVES 12

Macadamia Pie

Mauna Loa Macadamia Recipe Contest winner Dalo Dela Paz transforms a Southern classic into an Island treat.

1 1/4 cups light corn syrup
1 cup packed brown sugar
4 eggs
2 tablespoons melted butter
2 cups chopped Mauna Loa macadamias
1 ten-inch unbaked pie shell
Whipped cream, for garnish

Preheat oven to 350 degrees F.

In a large bowl, whisk together corn syrup, brown sugar and eggs until smooth. Stir in butter and macadamias. Pour into pie shell and bake for 50 to 60 minutes, or until knife inserted in the center comes out clean. Let pie cool completely before cutting. Serve with whipped cream.

SERVES 12

Macadamia and Chocolate Bavarois

Chef Fenton Lee at the Hyatt Regency Kauai developed this version of the elegant French dessert as a sophisticated finale to a formal dinner.

1 package unflavored gelatin	2 tablespoons macadamia liqueur
1 1/2 tablespoons cold water	1/2 cup chopped Mauna Loa
2 cups milk	macadamias
1/2 cup sugar, in all	2 cups heavy cream, whipped
5 egg yolks	Whipped cream, for garnish
5 ounces bittersweet chocolate, chopped	Chopped macadamias, for garnish

In a small bowl, dissolve gelatin in water and set aside.

In a heavy saucepan, whisk together milk and 1/4 cup of the sugar. In a bowl, whisk together egg yolks and remaining 1/4 cup sugar until mixture is pale in color and thick. Bring milk mixture to a boil over medium-high heat. As soon as the milk comes to a boil, pour half into egg yolks and whisk until blended. Pour egg yolk mixture back into the saucepan and whisk until blended. Simmer over low heat, stirring constantly with a wooden spoon, until mixture coats the back of the spoon. Remove from heat and whisk in the softened gelatin.

Divide mixture equally between 2 bowls. Whisk chopped chocolate into one of the bowls until smooth. Whisk macadamia liqueur and macadamias into the other bowl. Set both bowls in larger bowls filled with ice. Stir often to cool.

When both mixtures are very cool, divide the whipped cream and fold half into each until smooth. Layer in 6 large wine glasses. Cover and chill until firm, at least 4 hours.

Serve topped with whipped cream and a sprinkle of macadamias.

SERVES 6

Roasted Banana Cheesecake

Roasting intensifies and adds a wonderful depth of flavor to the bananas. This recipe is a must for card-carrying cheesecake afficionados.

3 ripe bananas, unpeeled

FILLING:
1 1/2 pounds cream cheese
3/4 cup sugar
5 eggs
1 tablespoon dark rum
1 teaspoon vanilla extract

CRUST:
1 1/2 cups (6 ounces) vanilla wafer
   cookie crumbs
1/2 cup finely chopped Mauna Loa
   macadamias
1/2 cup packed brown sugar
1/3 cup melted butter

Preheat oven to 400 degrees F.

Place the unpeeled bananas on a baking sheet and bake until they turn black all over, about 12 to 15 minutes. Cool, then remove and discard peels. Set aside.

For the crust: Combine the cookie crumbs, macadamias and brown sugar in the bowl of a food processor. Pulse a few times to mix ingredients. Add the butter and pulse to blend. Press mixture into the bottom of a 10-inch spring-form pan.

For the filling: In a large bowl, beat the cream cheese and sugar together until smooth, scraping the sides often. Add the eggs, one at a time, beating well after each addition. Add the roasted bananas, rum and vanilla and beat until smooth.

Reduce oven temperature to 350 degrees F.

Pour the batter into the prepared crust and place springform pan on a baking sheet. Bake for about 1 hour, or until cheesecake is very lightly golden and begins to pull away from the sides of the pan. Cool to room temperature, then cover and chill overnight.

SERVES 12

Macadamia Kona Coffee Brûlée

David Brown at the Hilton Hawaiian Village served me this creamy-smooth dessert with a cup of freshly brewed Kona coffee for a lightning strike of heady flavors.

2 cups heavy cream
3/4 cup finely chopped Mauna Loa macadamias, lightly toasted
2 teaspoons coarsely ground Kona coffee
1/2 vanilla bean, split lengthwise
1/3 cup sugar
4 egg yolks
3/4 cup sugar, divided

In a heavy saucepan, combine cream, macadamias, coffee and vanilla bean. Bring to a boil, then turn off heat and allow to steep for 1 hour.

Preheat oven to 325 degrees F.

In a large bowl, beat 1/3 cup sugar and egg yolks together until pale and thick. Strain cream mixture through a very fine sieve into the egg yolk mixture. Discard strained macadamias, ground coffee and vanilla bean. Stir until smooth. Pour mixture into 6 ramekins. Place ramekins in a shallow baking pan and add enough hot water to come half way up the sides of the ramekins. Bake for about 30 to 40 minutes, or until custard is set around the edges but still a little loose in the center. Remove from baking pan, let cool, then refrigerate until cold.

Preheat broiler.

When ready to serve, sprinkle 2 tablespoons sugar on top of each of the custards. Place under the broiler until the sugar caramelizes, taking care not to let them burn. Serve immediately.

SERVES 6

Black-Bottom Coconut Cream Tart with Macadamia Crust

This is a sophisticated but easy confection featuring a rich and buttery macadamia crust with a chocolate ganache layer and an old-fashioned coconut cream filling.

MACADAMIA CRUST:

1 1/2 cups all-purpose flour

1/2 cup cold butter, cut into small pieces

1/4 cup sugar

1 egg

1 teaspoon vanilla extract

1/8 teaspoon salt

1 cup finely ground Mauna Loa macadamias

CHOCOLATE GANACHE:

2 1/2 ounces bittersweet chocolate, chopped

1/4 cup heavy cream

COCONUT CREAM FILLING:

2 egg yolks

2 tablespoons cornstarch

1/3 cup sugar

1 cup milk, scalded

1 tablespoon butter

1/4 teaspoon vanilla extract

1/2 cup packed sweetened shredded coconut

GARNISH:

1/4 cup packed sweetened shredded coconut, lightly toasted

For the macadamia crust: In a large bowl, combine flour, butter, sugar, egg, vanilla and salt. Beat until mixture is well combined and crumbly. Stir in macadamias.

Press mixture firmly into the bottom and up the sides of a 9-inch tart pan with a removable bottom. Chill for 1 hour.

Preheat oven to 400 degrees F.

Bake tart crust in the middle of the oven for 20 to 25 minutes, or until golden brown. Remove from oven and cool.

For the chocolate ganache: Put chopped chocolate in a small bowl. In a small saucepan, bring cream to a boil. Immediately pour over chocolate and whisk until smooth. Spread chocolate ganache over the bottom of the crust.

For the coconut cream filling: In a small bowl, whisk the egg yolks lightly. In a small saucepan, whisk together cornstarch and sugar. Whisk in milk and cook over medium-high heat, whisking constantly, until slightly thickened. Pour about one quarter of the milk mixture into the egg yolks and whisk until blended. Pour egg yolk mixture back into the saucepan. Reduce heat to medium-low, and cook, whisking constantly, until thick. Remove from heat and whisk in butter and vanilla. Stir in coconut. Pour into tart, spreading the filling to the edges. Sprinkle with toasted coconut. Chill completely before serving.

SERVES 10

Macadamias and macadamia nut oil have a 1 to 1 ratio of omega-3 to omega-6 fatty acids. These essential fatty acids are responsible for the shine in our hair as well as our cardiovascular health. Macadamia oil is even healthier than olive oil, which has only a 1 to 5 ratio of omega-3 to omega-6 acids. Since most of us already receive more omega-6 fatty acids than we need, macadamia nuts and macadamia oil are ideal in helping to supply the proper amounts of omega-3 fatty acids.

Torta di Santa Maria

Catherine Whims created this flagship dessert for the Genoa Restaurant in Portland, Oregon.

TORTA:

3/4 cup raisins

1/2 cup orange liqueur

4 1/2 ounces semisweet chocolate

2/3 cup sugar

1/2 cup butter, softened

3 eggs

1/4 cup dry bread crumbs

1 cup chopped Mauna Loa macadamias, lightly toasted and finely ground

Zest from 1 orange, finely minced

GLAZE:

4 ounces semisweet chocolate

1 ounce unsweetened chocolate

2 tablespoons brewed espresso

1/4 cup butter, softened

Soak the raisins in the orange liqueur overnight.

Preheat the oven to 375 degrees F. Butter an 8-inch round cake pan, line the bottom with parchment paper and butter the parchment.

For the torta: In the top of a double boiler, melt the chocolate over simmering water. Remove from heat and let cool. In a large bowl, cream the sugar and butter together until fluffy. Add eggs, one at a time, beating well after each addition. Add the raisins and their liqueur, melted chocolate, macadamias, bread crumbs and orange zest and beat until well blended. Pour batter into prepared cake pan and bake for 30 to 35 minutes, or until edges start pulling away from the pan. The center should look slightly underdone. Cool 15 minutes in the pan, then run a knife around the edges and invert onto a rack. Let cool completely.

For the glaze: In the top of a double boiler, combine the semisweet chocolate, unsweetened chocolate and espresso. Melt slowly over simmering water and whisk until smooth. Remove from heat and whisk in the butter.

Place the rack on a baking sheet. Brush off any crumbs. With a small spatula, spread the glaze over the top and sides of the cake. Pour remaining glaze over the top evenly. Let cake stand for about 1 hour to allow the glaze to set.

SERVES 10

Macadamia and Strawberry Blancmange

Dating back to the Middle Ages, the French term "blancmange" literally means "white food" and thus perfectly describes this creamy confection. Less lyrically called "shape" in Britain, it provides light relief in the aftermath of a meaty meal.

1 cup finely ground Mauna Loa
   macadamias
1 1/4 cups water
2 packages unflavored gelatin
1/3 cup cold water
1 cup sugar

1/4 cup macadamia liqueur
1 cup milk
1 cup heavy cream
8 ounces strawberries, hulled and diced
Perfect strawberries, for garnish

Lightly oil a 6-cup ring mold and wipe out excess oil.

In a small bowl, stir together ground macadamias and 1 1/4 cups water. Let stand for 1 hour.

Place a colander in a large bowl. Lay a damp tea towel in the colander. Pour the macadamia mixture into the center of the towel, allowing the liquid to strain through. Bring up the sides of the towel and twist around the macadamias, squeezing out as much liquid as possible. Discard macadamias.

In a small bowl, soften the gelatin in the 1/3 cup water. Set aside.

In a saucepan, combine the macadamia liquid, sugar and macadamia liqueur. Bring to a boil, then remove from heat and whisk in the softened gelatin. Pour mixture into a large bowl and place in a larger bowl of ice.

In the same saucepan, bring milk to a boil. Stir milk into macadamia mixture. Stir until completely cool.

Whip cream until stiff, then gently fold into the cooled macadamia mixture. Fold in strawberries. Pour into prepared mold, cover with plastic wrap and chill overnight.

To serve, dip mold in hot water for a moment. Invert onto a serving plate and carefully remove mold. Decorate with strawberries.

SERVES 10

Banana Gyoza

The talented Scott Lutey at the Napili Kai Beach Club in Lahaina, gave me this exotic, though surprisingly easy Asian dessert. Fresh gyoza wrappers can be found in the Asian section of most larger supermarkets. In a pinch, you may substitute wonton wrappers.

2 cups diced bananas

1/2 cup finely chopped Mauna Loa macadamias

1/4 cup semisweet chocolate chips

1 tablespoon cornstarch

1 tablespoon cold water

16 gyoza wrappers

3 tablespoons Mauna Loa Macadamia Oil

Vanilla ice cream

1/4 cup raspberries

2 tablespoons chopped candied ginger

In a large bowl, stir together bananas, macadamias and chocolate chips. Set this filling aside. In a small bowl, stir together the cornstarch and water. Place 1 1/2 tablespoons of the banana filling in the middle of a gyoza wrapper. Brush the edges of the wrapper with the cornstarch mixture. Fold over and press edges together to seal. Repeat procedure until all ingredients are used.

In a large nonstick skillet, heat oil over medium-high heat. Add the gyozas and sauté until golden on both sides. Drain on paper towels. Serve hot gyozas with vanilla ice cream, raspberries and candied ginger.

SERVES 4

Hawaii Prince Macadamia Chocolate Pie

Chef Andre Fusero at the Hawaii Prince Hotel, Waikiki, graciously shared the secrets to his sinfully rich, world-class pie.

1 nine-inch prebaked pie shell

CARAMEL LAYER:

1/2 cup sugar

2 tablespoons water

1 tablespoon corn syrup

3 tablespoons heavy cream

2 tablespoons butter

1 1/4 cups chopped Mauna Loa macadamias, lightly toasted

CHOCOLATE FILLING:

7 tablespoons sour cream

1 egg

1 egg yolk

2 tablespoons heavy cream

2 tablespoons sugar

2 ounces bittersweet chocolate, chopped

TOPPING:

1 1/2 cups heavy cream

2 tablespoons sugar

For the caramel layer: In a heavy saucepan, whisk together sugar, water and corn syrup. Bring to a boil over high heat until the sugar begins to caramelize. Swirl the pan gently to allow the syrup to caramelize evenly. When caramel is deep brown, remove from heat. Stir in the cream and butter until smooth. Stir in the macadamias. Pour into pie shell and chill.

For the chocolate filling: In the top of a double boiler, whisk together sour cream, egg, egg yolk, heavy cream and sugar. Cook over simmering water, stirring constantly, until mixture becomes thick enough to coat the back of a spoon. Remove from heat and whisk in chocolate until smooth. Pour on top of the caramel layer. Chill.

For the topping: In a large bowl, whip cream until soft peaks form. Beat in sugar. Spread over pie and sprinkle with chocolate shavings. Serve immediately.

SERVES 8

Nutty Peaches

Elizabeth Thomas, of the Elizabeth Thomas Cooking School in Berkeley, California, offers this lovely way to savor the all-too-short season of tree-ripened peaches.

4 ripe peaches
1/4 cup freshly squeezed orange juice
1/4 cup packed brown sugar
2 tablespoons orange liqueur
1/2 cup heavy cream
1/4 cup sour cream
2 tablespoons sugar
1/2 cup chopped Mauna Loa macadamias

Peel, pit and slice the peaches. Distribute evenly between 6 pretty glass dishes. In a bowl, whisk together orange juice, brown sugar and liqueur until sugar dissolves. Pour over the peaches. In a bowl, whip the cream just until stiff. In a small bowl, whisk the sour cream with the sugar, then fold into the whipped cream. Spoon the cream over the peaches and sprinkle with macadamias.

SERVES 6

Espresso Cheesecake

🍩 *My husband's prediction—this is destined to become every coffee lover's ultimate cheesecake recipe.*

CRUST:

1 1/2 cups (6 ounces) chocolate cookie crumbs

1/4 cup sugar

1/3 cup melted butter

FILLING:

1 1/2 pounds cream cheese

1 1/4 cups sugar

2 tablespoons all-purpose flour

3 eggs

3/4 cup heavy cream

1/4 cup brewed espresso

1/2 teaspoon freshly squeezed lemon juice

1/2 teaspoon vanilla extract

CHOCOLATE GLAZE:

3/4 cup heavy cream

1 teaspoon vanilla extract

1 cup semisweet chocolate chips

Chocolate covered macadamias, for garnish

1/2 cup finely chopped Mauna Loa macadamias

🍩 Preheat oven to 350 degrees F.

For the crust: Place the cookie crumbs and sugar in the bowl of a food processor. Pulse a few times to mix ingredients. Add the melted butter and pulse to blend. Press the mixture into the bottom of a 10-inch springform pan.

For the filling: In a large bowl, beat the cream cheese, sugar and flour together until smooth, scraping the sides often. Add the eggs, one at a time, beating well after each addition. Beat in the cream, espresso, lemon juice and vanilla until smooth.

Pour batter into the prepared crust and place springform pan on a baking sheet. Bake for about 45 minutes, or until cheesecake is very lightly golden and begins to pull away from the sides of the pan. Cool to room temperature, then cover and chill overnight.

For the chocolate glaze: In a small saucepan, bring the cream and vanilla to a boil. Remove from heat and whisk in the chocolate chips until smooth. Let cool until warm but still pourable.

Remove cheesecake from the refrigerator. Pour glaze evenly over the top of cheesecake. Press chocolate covered macadamias gently into the glaze around the edge of the cheesecake. Chill for 1 hour in the refrigerator to allow the glaze to set.

Remove the cheesecake from the refrigerator. Carefully remove the band of the springform pan and place cheesecake on a baking sheet. Press maca-damias into the side of the cheesecake. Carefully slide a long spatula under the crust of the cheesecake and slide onto a serving platter.

SERVES 12

*Macadamia nut oil is even lower in
saturated fats than olive oil.*

Iced Lemon Macadamia Pound Cake

🍥 *This is a dazzling little cake to serve in wedges with tea. The intense lemon flavor is mellowed by the creamy flavor of the macadamias.*

POUND CAKE:
1 cup chopped Mauna Loa
   macadamias

1 cup sugar

1 cup butter, softened

4 eggs

1/4 cup freshly squeezed lemon juice

1 tablespoon finely minced lemon
   zest

1 cup all-purpose flour

1 teaspoon baking powder

1/4 teaspoon salt

ICING:
1 1/2 cups powdered sugar

3 tablespoons freshly squeezed lemon juice

8 candied violets, for garnish

🍥 Preheat the oven to 350 degrees F. Butter and flour a 9-inch round cake pan.

For the pound cake: In the bowl of a food processor, combine the macadamias and sugar and process until finely ground. In a large bowl, cream the butter and macadamia mixture until light and fluffy, scraping the sides of the bowl often. Add the eggs, one at a time, beating well after each addition. Beat in the lemon juice and zest. Sift the flour, baking powder and salt over the batter and beat until smooth.

Pour batter into the prepared pan and bake for 40 to 45 minutes, or until a toothpick inserted in the center comes out clean. Cool for 15 minutes in the pan, then run a knife around the edges and invert onto a rack. Cool completely.

For the icing: Whisk the powdered sugar and lemon juice together until completely smooth.

Place the rack on a baking sheet. Brush off any crumbs. With a small spatula, spread icing over the top and sides of the cake. Wait about 15 minutes and ice the sides again. Pour remaining icing over the top evenly. Place candied violets, evenly spaced, around the edge of the cake. Let cake stand about 1 hour to allow the icing to harden.

SERVES 8

Macnut Flan

This splendid dessert combining caramel, macadamias and bittersweet chocolate, bears little resemblance to a flan, but remains a unanimous favorite at one of Maui's most celebrated restaurants, David Paul's Lahaina Grill.

CRUST:

1 1/2 cups all-purpose flour

3 tablespoons powdered sugar

1/2 teaspoon salt

2/3 cup cold butter, cut into small pieces

1 egg yolk

1 1/2 teaspoons heavy cream

1 1/2 teaspoons vanilla extract

FILLING:

1/4 cup butter

1/2 cup sugar

1/2 cup chopped Mauna Loa macadamias

1/4 cup heavy cream

TOPPING:

1 cup heavy cream

2 tablespoons powdered sugar

1/2 teaspoon vanilla extract

MOUSSE:

1/2 cup chopped bittersweet chocolate

1/4 cup heavy cream

3/4 cup sour cream

Chocolate curls, for garnish

White chocolate curls, for garnish

Macadamias, for garnish

❧ Lightly oil a 9-inch tart pan with a removable bottom.

For the crust: In a large bowl, stir together flour, powdered sugar and salt. Cut in the butter until mixture resembles coarse meal. In a small bowl, whisk together the egg yolk, cream and vanilla. Stir into flour mixture until dough holds together. Gather dough into a ball and flatten into a disc. Cover with plastic wrap and chill.

Turn dough out onto a lightly floured surface and roll out to fit tart pan. Prick all over with a fork. Freeze for about 15 minutes.

Preheat oven to 400 degrees F.

Bake tart shell for about 20 minutes, or until golden brown. Remove from oven and cool in pan on a rack.

For the filling: In a heavy saucepan, melt butter and sugar together over medium heat, stirring often until sugar dissolves. Bring to a boil over high heat until sugar starts to caramelize. Swirl pan gently to allow the syrup to caramelize evenly to a deep golden brown. Remove from heat and stir in macadamias and cream. Spread into the bottom of tart shell evenly and freeze.

For the topping: In a large bowl, beat the cream until stiff. Beat in the sugar and vanilla. Divide in half and set aside in the refrigerator.

For the mousse: Place the chopped chocolate in a large bowl. In a small saucepan, bring the cream to a boil and pour over the chocolate. Whisk until smooth. Add the sour cream and whisk just until smooth. Take half of the reserved topping mixture and carefully fold into the chocolate mixture taking care not to deflate mixture. Spread the mousse evenly over the filling.

Spread remaining topping over the mousse and chill for at least 3 hours before serving. To serve, remove tart from pan and place on a serving platter. Garnish with chocolate curls, white chocolate curls and sprinkle with macadamias.

SERVES 10

Chocolate Macadamia Truffle Torte

Glenn Chu at Indigo Restaurant in Honolulu showcases the velvety richness of macadamias in a dense flourless chocolate cake.

1 pound plus 4 ounces dark chocolate, chopped
1 cup butter
1 cup chopped Mauna Loa macadamias, lightly toasted
5 eggs
Cocoa powder, for garnish

Preheat oven to 300 degrees F. Generously butter a 9-inch springform pan.

In the top of a double boiler, melt the chocolate and butter together over simmering water. Remove from heat and stir in macadamias. Let cool.

In a large bowl, beat eggs until light and foamy. Gently fold chocolate mixture into eggs. Do not over mix. Pour batter into prepared pan and bake for about 20 to 30 minutes, or until almost set in the middle. Cool in the pan, then cover and refrigerate.

Remove from pan and place on serving platter. Dust with cocoa powder.

SERVES 10

Paradise Cake

This exotic variation on the traditional fruitcake is laden with tropical fruit and macadamias. Try it as an energizing breakfast or as a rejuvenating afternoon snack.

6 eggs
1 cup sugar
$^1/4$ cup honey
3 tablespoons Mauna Loa Macadamia Oil
1 tablespoon vanilla extract
$1^1/3$ cups all-purpose flour
$2^1/2$ teaspoons baking powder
1 teaspoon salt
2 cups sweetened shredded coconut
10 ounces dried pineapple, finely diced
1 cup chopped Mauna Loa macadamias
1 cup finely chopped Mauna Loa macadamias

Preheat oven to 300 degrees F. Line the bottom of an angel food cake pan with a removable bottom with parchment paper, then oil the bottom and sides of pan.

In a large bowl, beat eggs and sugar together until frothy. Beat in honey, oil and vanilla until smooth. Add flour, baking powder and salt and beat until smooth. Stir in coconut, pineapple and macadamias until well combined.

Pour batter into prepared pan and bake for about 1 hour and 10 minutes or until toothpick inserted in the center comes out clean. Cool in the pan then run a knife around the edge of the pan and around the center hole to loosen the cake. Invert onto a serving plate and peel off parchment.

SERVES 12

Frozen Honey and Macadamia Nougat with Bittersweet Chocolate Sauce

Although initially inspired by Middle Eastern cuisine, international borders melt away in the wake of this "dessert storm." Definitely not for the faint-hearted.

PRALINE:
1 cup chopped Mauna Loa macadamias

1/2 cup sugar

1/4 cup water

CRÈME ANGLAISE:
3 egg yolks

1/4 cup honey

1 cup milk

1 teaspoon vanilla extract

ITALIAN MERINGUE:
1 1/4 cups sugar

1/4 cup water

4 egg whites

1/8 teaspoon salt

BITTERSWEET CHOCOLATE SAUCE:
1 cup heavy cream

1 teaspoon vanilla extract

9 ounces bittersweet chocolate, chopped

Preheat the oven to 400 degrees F. Line a 9 x 5-inch loaf pan with parchment paper and oil lightly.

For the praline: Spread macadamias on a baking sheet and toast until they are just turning golden, about 3 to 4 minutes. In a small sauce pan, bring sugar and water to a boil, swirling the pan often to blend. Cook until sugar caramelizes and turns deep golden brown. Stir in the hot macadamias. Pour onto a lightly oiled baking sheet and spread out with an oiled spoon. Allow to cool completely, then chop coarsely. Set aside.

For the crème Anglaise: In a small bowl, whisk the egg yolks lightly. In a medium saucepan, bring the milk, honey and vanilla to a simmer over medium heat. As soon as the milk starts to boil, pour half into the egg yolks and whisk until blended. Pour the egg yolk mixture back into the saucepan and whisk until blended. Simmer over low heat, stirring constantly with a wooden spoon, until mixture coats the back of the spoon. Strain through a fine sieve into a bowl placed inside a larger bowl filled with ice. Stir occasionally until cool. Set aside.

For the Italian meringue: Combine the sugar and water in a saucepan and simmer over low heat until sugar dissolves. Raise the heat to high and cook until it reaches 244 degrees F. While the sugar is cooking, beat the egg whites and salt until stiff. The sugar mixture and the egg whites should be ready at the same time. Pour the hot sugar syrup in a slow, thin, steady stream into the egg whites, beating constantly. Continue beating until meringue is cool.

Gently fold crème Anglaise and 1 cup of the reserved praline into the meringue, taking care not to deflate the mixture. Spoon mixture into the prepared pan and freeze overnight.

For the bittersweet chocolate sauce: In a small saucepan, bring the cream and vanilla to a boil. Remove from heat and whisk in the chocolate until very smooth.

To serve, unmold frozen nougat onto a chilled serving platter and remove parchment paper. Cut into slices with a sharp knife dipped in warm water. Place on chilled plates. Sprinkle reserved praline over the top. Ladle some of the bittersweet chocolate sauce over and serve immediately.

SERVES 10

Orange and Macadamia Praline Tiramisu

This refined version of the great Italian favorite features a silky orange filling with the special crunch of macadamia praline.

CAKE:

6 eggs, separated

1/8 teaspoon salt

2/3 cup sugar

2/3 cup all-purpose flour

PRALINE:

1 cup chopped Mauna Loa
    macadamias

1/2 cup sugar

1/4 cup water

SYRUP:

1 cup strained fresh orange juice

1/3 cup orange liqueur

1/3 cup sugar

FILLING:

4 egg yolks

2/3 cup sugar

8 ounces mascarpone cheese

1 cup heavy cream

1 tablespoon minced orange zest

Preheat oven to 400 degrees F. Butter and flour two 8-inch round cake pans.

For the cake: In a large bowl, beat egg whites with the salt to soft peaks. Continue beating and gradually add sugar in a steady stream. Beat until stiff. Gently fold in egg yolks. Sift flour over egg white mixture and gently fold together, taking care not to deflate mixture. Pour batter into prepared pans and bake for about 15 to 20 minutes, or until a toothpick inserted in the center comes out clean and cake is golden brown. Remove from oven and cool completely on a rack.

For the praline: Spread macadamias on a baking sheet and toast until they are just turning golden, about 3 to 4 minutes.

In a small saucepan, bring sugar and water to a boil, swirling the pan often to blend. Cook until sugar caramelizes and turns deep golden brown. Stir in the hot macadamias. Pour onto a lightly oiled baking sheet and spread with an oiled spoon. Allow to cool completely then chop coarsely. Measure out 1 cup of praline and reserve the rest for garnish.

For the syrup: In a small saucepan, reduce the orange juice by half over medium heat. Add the liqueur and sugar and bring to a boil, then reduce heat to medium and simmer until sugar completely dissolves. Allow to cool.

For the filling: In a large bowl, beat the egg yolks and sugar until thick and pale in color. In a separate bowl, beat the mascarpone with the cream until smooth. Add the mascarpone mixture to the sugar mixture and beat until well blended. Stir in the orange zest and 1 cup of the praline.

To assemble: Slice both cakes in half horizontally. Place the top layer of one of the cakes, cut side up, in the bottom of a straight-sided, glass trifle dish. Brush with one quarter of the syrup. Spoon one quarter of the filling on top. Repeat with the remaining layers, ending with the filling. Cover and chill for at least 4 hours before serving. Sprinkle reserved praline around the edge of the bowl.

SERVES 10

Macadamias have the same total fat content as pecans, but contain nearly double the amount of monounsaturated fatty acids. In fact, of all of the most common nuts, macadamias are highest in monounsaturated fats and lowest in saturated fats.

Danish Macadamia Puff

🍃 *A glorious choice for a Sunday brunch, the dense macadamia filling never overpowers the exceptionally delicate crust.*

CRUST:

1 cup all-purpose flour

1/4 cup sugar

1/2 cup cold butter, cut into small pieces

2 tablespoons cold water

FILLING:

1 cup water

1/2 cup butter

1/4 cup sugar

1 tablespoon macadamia liqueur

1 cup all-purpose flour

3 eggs, lightly beaten

7 ounces Macadamia Paste, page 159

TOPPING:

1 1/2 cups powdered sugar

2 teaspoons butter, softened

1 1/2 teaspoons vanilla extract

1 to 2 tablespoons hot water

1/4 cup finely chopped Mauna Loa macadamias

🍃 Preheat oven to 350 degrees F.

For the crust: In a large bowl, combine flour and sugar. Cut in the butter until the mixture resembles coarse meal. Sprinkle cold water over and combine just until the dough holds together. Gather dough into a ball, wrap in plastic wrap, form into a disc and chill for 30 minutes. Turn dough out onto a lightly floured surface and roll out to a 12-inch circle. Place on a pizza pan and pinch the edges decoratively. Chill.

For the filling: In a saucepan, combine water, butter, sugar and macadamia liqueur. Bring to a simmer over low heat and stir with a wooden spoon until butter melts. Increase heat to high and bring to a boil. Remove pan from heat and add flour all at once. Beat vigorously until all flour is incorporated and mixture pulls away from the sides of the pan and forms a ball. Add the eggs and beat until the eggs are incorporated and mixture is smooth and glossy.

Remove crust from refrigerator. Cut the macadamia paste into small pieces and put them evenly over the crust. Spread filling mixture completely over the macadamia paste, and seal to the edge of the crust. Bake for about 45 minutes, or until topping is golden brown. The custard will puff up and then fall. Remove from oven and let cool.

For the topping: Combine powdered sugar, butter, vanilla and hot water and stir until smooth. Drizzle over cooled custard. Sprinkle the macadamias over the top. Cut into thin wedges.

SERVES 12

Out of the way, olive oil! Macadamia oil is more monounsaturated than olive oil. Macadamia oil is 80 percent monounsaturated, while olive oil is only 74 percent. Another of our favorites, canola oil is a mere 58 percent monounsaturated!

Chocolate Macadamia Wontons

Chocolate wontons? You bet! And nobody makes them like Glenn Chu at Indigo in Honolulu.

40 square wonton wrappers
1 egg, beaten
1 Chocolate Macadamia Truffle Torte, page 144
Oil for deep frying
Powdered sugar

Place 1 teaspoon of the torte in the middle of a wonton wrapper. Brush edges with egg. Fold over and press edges together to make a triangle. Bring bottom corners together, brush with egg and seal. Repeat procedure. Place wontons on a baking sheet without touching each other and freeze for at least 2 hours.

Heat oil to 365 degrees F. Deep fry in batches until golden brown. Drain on paper towels. Dust with powdered sugar and serve immediately.

SERVES 10

Sweet Macadamia Cake with Raspberries

This is a delightful tea cake that is quick and simple to prepare and provides the perfect counterpoint for ripe, tart-sweet raspberries.

1 cup sugar
1 cup finely chopped Mauna Loa macadamias
1/2 cup butter, softened
3 eggs
1/2 teaspoon vanilla extract
1/4 cup all-purpose flour
1 teaspoon baking powder
1/8 teaspoon salt
Powdered sugar
Fresh raspberries

Preheat oven to 350 degrees F. Lightly oil a 9-inch round cake pan, line the bottom with parchment paper and oil the parchment.

In the bowl of a food processor, combine the sugar and macadamias and process until finely ground. Pour mixture into a large bowl. Add butter and beat until well blended. Add eggs, one at a time, beating well after each addition. Beat in vanilla. Add flour, baking powder and salt and beat until smooth. Pour batter into prepared pan and bake for 35 to 40 minutes, or until the cake has completely pulled away from the edges of the pan. Cool in the pan, then invert onto a serving plate and dust with powdered sugar. Serve in thin wedges with raspberries.

SERVES 10

Pumpkin Cheesecake with Macadamia Gingersnap Crust

My husband Richard adores pumpkin pie and I'm crazy for cheesecake. To keep the peace we had to invent the perfect compromise. In fact, it's the best of both worlds that's absolutely out of this world!

CRUST:
1 1/2 cups (6 ounces) gingersnap crumbs
1/2 cup finely chopped Mauna Loa macadamias
1/4 cup packed brown sugar
1/3 cup melted butter

FILLING:
1 pound cream cheese
8 ounces mascarpone cheese
1 cup sugar
1 cup pumpkin
3 eggs
2 teaspoons cinnamon
1 teaspoon ground ginger

Preheat oven to 350 degrees F.

For the crust: Place the gingersnap crumbs, macadamias and brown sugar in the bowl of a food processor. Pulse a few times to mix ingredients. Add the melted butter and pulse to blend. Press the mixture into the bottom of a 10-inch springform pan.

For the filling: In a large bowl, beat the cream cheese, mascarpone and sugar together until smooth, scraping the sides often. Add pumpkin and beat until smooth. Add the eggs, one at a time, beating well after each addition. Add the cinnamon and ginger and beat until smooth.

Pour batter into the prepared crust and place springform pan on a baking sheet. Bake for 45 to 50 minutes, or until cheesecake is very lightly golden and begins to pull away from the sides of the pan. Cool to room temperature, then cover and chill overnight.

SERVES 12

Macadamia and Raspberry Tart

This is one of my favorite breakfast pastries, either on its own, or as an admittedly decadant accompaniment to eggs Benedict.

SWEET PASTRY DOUGH:

1 1/3 cups all-purpose flour

3 tablespoons sugar

1/4 teaspoon salt

1/2 cup cold butter, cut into small pieces

1 large egg

2 tablespoons cold water

1 teaspoon vanilla extract

FILLING:

1 cup finely chopped Mauna Loa macadamias

1/2 cup sugar

4 eggs

1/2 cup all-purpose flour

3/4 cup raspberry jam

1/2 cup chopped Mauna Loa macadamias

Preheat oven to 350 degrees F.

For the sweet pastry dough: In a large bowl, stir together flour, sugar and salt. Cut in the butter until mixture resembles coarse meal. In a small bowl, whisk together the egg, water and vanilla. Stir into flour mixture until dough holds together. Gather dough into a ball, wrap it in plastic wrap, form into a disc and chill for about 30 minutes.

Turn dough out onto a lightly floured surface and roll out to fit a 10-inch tart pan with a removable bottom. Chill.

For the filling: In the bowl of a food processor, combine the 1 cup of macadamias and sugar and process until finely ground. Pour mixture into a large bowl. Add eggs, one at a time, beating well after each addition. Add flour and beat until smooth.

Spread raspberry jam over the bottom of the crust. Spread the macadamia mixture evenly over the jam. Sprinkle the 1/2 cup macadamias on top. Bake for 35 to 40 minutes, or until golden. Cool completely before removing tart from the pan.

SERVES 12

Hawaiian Success

Gerard Reversade of Gerard's at the Plantation Inn on Maui, builds fragile layers of macadamia meringue and fills them with a lusty chocolate and coffee ganache.

MERINGUE LAYERS:

8 egg whites

1 cup plus 1 tablespoon sugar

3/4 cup finely chopped Mauna Loa macadamias

CHOCOLATE AND COFFEE GANACHE:

12 ounces dark chocolate, chopped

3 tablespoons butter

1 tablespoon strong brewed coffee

2/3 cup heavy cream

1/4 cup coarsely ground coffee

1/4 cup sugar

1/2 cup chopped Mauna Loa macadamias, for garnish

Cocoa powder, for garnish

Preheat oven to 250 degrees F. Butter and flour two baking sheets. Using an 8-inch round cake pan as a guide, mark three circles on the baking sheets with the tip of a sharp knife.

For the meringue layers: In a large bowl, beat the egg whites until they hold soft peaks. Beat in 1 cup sugar, a little at a time, until stiff and glossy. Mix the remaining 1 tablespoon sugar with the macadamias. Gently fold macadamia mixture into egg white mixture taking care not to overmix. Fill a pastry bag fitted with a 1/2-inch plain tip with the meringue. Starting from the middle of the circles, pipe a continuous spiral of meringue until the outlines are filled. Bake for about 45 minutes, or until crisp and lightly colored. Remove from oven and cool on the baking sheets.

For the chocolate and coffee ganache: In a large bowl, combine chocolate, butter and brewed coffee. Set aside.

In a small saucepan, bring the cream to a boil. Stir in the ground coffee and sugar and remove from heat. Cover and let infuse for 5 minutes. Strain hot cream mixture through a very fine sieve into the chocolate mixture and whisk until smooth. Discard coffee grounds. Cool, then cover and chill for at least 2 hours. Remove ganache from refrigerator and beat vigorously until the color has lightened and the texture is creamy.

Place a meringue layer on a serving plate. Carefully spread one third of the ganache on top, taking care not to break the fragile meringues. Continue with remaining meringue layers and ganache. Sprinkle $^1/_2$ cup macadamias on top and dust with cocoa powder.

SERVES 8

Macadamia Paste

This basic macadamia paste recipe is the versatile foundation for many wonderful fillings. Make it ahead of time and store it frozen.

2 cups chopped Mauna Loa macadamias
$1^1/_3$ cups sugar
1 egg white

In the bowl of a food processor, combine macadamias and sugar. Process until finely ground. Add egg white and continue to process until mixture forms a grainy paste. Freeze in 7-ounce portions.

MAKES ABOUT 21 OUNCES
OR ABOUT $2^1/_4$ PACKED CUPS

Macadamia Cheesecake

Cheesecake purists may be reluctant to try this variation, but an adventurous spirit will be well rewarded.

CRUST:
1 1/2 cups (6 ounces) amaretti cookie crumbs
1/2 cup finely chopped Mauna Loa macadamias
1/2 cup packed brown sugar
1/3 cup melted butter

FILLING:
1 1/2 pounds cream cheese
3/4 cup sugar
1 tablespoon all-purpose flour
4 eggs
1/3 cup macadamia liqueur
1 teaspoon vanilla extract

Preheat oven to 350 degrees F.

For the crust: Combine the cookie crumbs, macadamias and brown sugar in the bowl of a food processor. Pulse a few times to mix ingredients. Add the butter and pulse to blend. Press mixture into the bottom of a 10-inch spring-form pan.

For the filling: In a large bowl, beat the cream cheese, sugar and flour together until smooth, scraping the sides often. Add the eggs, one at a time, beating well after each addition. Add the macadamia liqueur and vanilla and beat until smooth.

Pour the batter into the prepared crust and place springform pan on a baking sheet. Bake for about 1 hour, or until cheesecake is very lightly golden and begins to pull away from the sides of the pan. Cool to room temperature, then cover and chill overnight.

SERVES 12

Conversions

LIQUID
1 tablespoon = 15 milliliters
1/2 cup = 4 fluid ounces = 125 milliliters
1 cup = 8 fluid ounces = 250 milliliters

DRY
1/4 cup = 4 tablespoons = 2 ounces = 60 grams
1 cup = 1/2 pound = 8 ounces = 250 grams

FLOUR
1/2 cup = 60 grams
1 cup = 4 ounces = 125 grams

TEMPERATURE
400 degrees F = 200 degrees C = gas mark 6
375 degrees F = 190 degrees C = gas mark 5
350 degrees F = 175 degrees C = gas mark 4

MISCELLANEOUS
2 tablespoons butter = 1 ounce = 30 grams
1 inch = 2.5 centimeters
all purpose flour = plain flour
baking soda = bicarbonate of soda
brown sugar = demerara sugar
confectioners' sugar = icing sugar
heavy cream = double cream
molasses = black treacle
raisins = sultanas
rolled oats = oat flakes
semisweet chocolate = plain chocolate
sugar = caster sugar

Macadamia nut oil is even lower in saturated fats than olive oil.

COMPOSITION OF MACADAMIAS:
(per 100 grams)

Water: 2.88 grams

Calories: 702

Protein: 8.3%

Fat: 73.72%

Fiber: 5.28%

VITAMINS:

Thiamin: 0.35 mg

Riboflavin: 0.11 mg

Niacin: 2.14 mg

MINERALS:

Calcium: 70 mg

Iron: 2.43 mg

Magnesium: 116 mg

Phosphorus: 136 mg

Sodium: 5 mg

Zinc: 1.71 mg

Copper: 0.3 mg

- Macadamia oil has no more calories than any other fat, costs only about as much as extra virgin olive oil and can be used anywhere oil is called for.

- If all you have are the salted macadamias, here's a tip for removing the salt: Place the salted macadamias in a large strainer, rinse for about 10 seconds with warm water then drain. Transfer the nuts to a baking sheet and dry them at 250 degrees F, shaking the baking sheet occasionally. Transfer to a plate and let them cool completely.

- The oil in macadamias has a higher level of the all-important omega-3 fatty acid even than olive oil. Coupled with its extremely high smoke point, higher than any other food oil, macadamia oil is the perfect oil for healthful and flavorful stir-frying, sautéeing, immersion-frying and grilling.

- A University of Hawaii study showed that a diet high in macadamias caused a significant drop in LDL cholesterol without affecting the HDL cholesterol. Other diets which were merely low-fat, without the benefits of macadamias, reduced HDL cholesterol.

PHOTO CREDITS

Front Cover: Macadamias and Horse Spirit House by Larry Kunkel Photography and Banana Leaf by Ann Cecil, Stock Photos Hawaii

page ii: Kalalau Valley, Kauai by Ann Cecil, Stock Photos Hawaii

page iv: Yellow Plumerias by Ann Cecil, Stock Photos Hawaii

page vi: Macadamias by John De Mello, Stock Photos Hawaii

page vii: Coconut Palms, Kauai by Ann Cecil, Stock Photos Hawaii

page viii: Nanue Waterfall, Hamakua Coast, Big Island by Ann Cecil, Stock Photos Hawaii

page 2 : Kohala Coast, Big Island by John De Mello, Stock Photos Hawaii

page 4: Cream of Tomato Soup with Onion & Garlic Macadamias by Larry Kunkel Photography and Pandanus Plant, Waimea Falls, Oahu by Ann Cecil, Stock Photos Hawaii

page 9: Waikoloa Sunset, Big Island by Ann Cecil, Stock Photos Hawaii

page 10: Onion & Garlic Macadamias by Larry Kunkel Photography and Dieffenbachia Leaf by Craig Fineman, Stock Photos Hawaii

page 15: Macadamia Tree Nursery, Big Island by John Penisten Photography

page 17: Kihei Sunset, Maui by John De Mello, Stock Photos Hawaii

page 19: Macadamias, Big Island by John De Mello, Stock Photos Hawaii

page 21: Main Vent Eruption Mauna Loa Volcano, Big Island by John Penisten Photography

page 22: Rainbow and Coconut Palms, Oahu by Ann Cecil, Stock Photos Hawaii

page 25: Thai Corn Fritters by Larry Kunkel Photography and Traveler's Palm by Jack McCarty, Stock Photos Hawaii

page 29: Ke'e Beach, Na Pali Coast, Kauai by Ann Cecil, Stock Photos Hawaii

page 30: Waterfall, Hana, Maui by David Olsen, Stock Photos Hawaii

page 32: Sea Bass & Macadamias with Warm Lemon Curry Vinaigrette by Larry Kunkel and Woven Lauhala Mat by Ann Cecil, Stock Photos Hawaii

page 37: Ala Wai Boat Harbor, Oahu by Ann Cecil, Stock Photos Hawaii

page 38: Macadamia-Crusted Tofu with Noodles by Larry Kunkel Photography and Banana Leaf by Ann Cecil, Stock Photos Hawaii

page 43: Macadamia Harvest, Big Island by John De Mello, Stock Photos Hawaii

page 45: Lanikai Beach, Oahu by Ann Cecil, Stock Photos Hawaii

page 47: Macadamia Tree, Big Island by John De Mello, Stock Photos Hawaii

page 51: Vietnamese Cellophane Noodle Salad with Grilled Shrimp by Larry Kunkel Photography and Black Sand by Mike Horikawa, Stock Photos Hawaii

page 53: Lava Flow to the Sea, Kamoamoa, Big Island by John Penisten Photography

page 54: Beach with Palm Shadow and Beach Chair by Sun Star, Stock Photos Hawaii

page 56: Ocean and Sky by Sun Star, Stock Photos Hawaii

page 63: Black Point Sunset, Oahu by Ann Cecil, Stock Photos Hawaii

page 64: Waimanalo Coast, Oahu by Ann Cecil, Stock Photos Hawaii

page 66: Macadamia & Currant Scones by Larry Kunkel Photography and Waimea Bay, Oahu by Ann Cecil, Stock Photos Hawaii

page 71: Big Beach, Maui by David Olsen, Stock Photos Hawaii

page 72: Macadamia Cheesecake & Macadamia Braid by Larry Kunkel Photography and Lauhala Mat by Ann Cecil, Stock Photos Hawaii

page 75: Waimea Bay, Oahu by Chris Dyball, Stock Photos Hawaii

page 76: Message in a Bottle by Sun Star, Stock Photos Hawaii

page 79: Macadamia Sticky Buns by Larry Kunkel Phtography and Starfish and Shells by Ann Cecil, Stock Photos Hawaii

page 80: Macadamias, Big Island by John De Mello, Stock Photos Hawaii

page 81: Taro Fields, Hanalei, Kauai by David Olsen, Stock Photos Hawaii

page 82: Reflected Coconut Palms by John De Mello, Stock Photos, Hawaii

page 84: Macadamia Coconut Icebox Cookies, Chocolate Macadamia Shortbread Cookies & Chocolate-Toppped Mocha Cookies by Larry Kunkel Photography and Leaf by Dwayne Reed, Stock Photos Hawaii

page 89: Palm Fronds by Ann Cecil, Stock Photos Hawaii

page 90: Mauna Loa Macadamia Brittle, Chocolate Macadamia Biscotti, Chocolate Macadamia Fudge & Macadamia Cheesecake Brownie by Larry Kunkel Photography and Honomano, Maui by David Olsen, Stock Photos Hawaii

page 93: Lava Flowing to the Sea, Big Island by Ann Cecil, Stock Photos Hawaii

page 94: Lava Flowing into the Sea, Kamoamoa, Big Island by John Penisten Photography

page 99: Twelve-foot Surf at the Banzai Pipeline, North Shore, Oahu by Ann Cecil, Stock Photos Hawaii

page 103: Wailua Falls, Maui by J. Davis, Stock Photos Hawaii

page 104: Silverswords, Haleakala, Maui by David Olsen, Stock Photos Hawaii

page 107: Macadamia Tree, Big Island by John Penisten Photography

page 109: Kapalua Coast, Maui by Ann Cecil, Stock Photos Hawaii

page 112: Kilauea Volcano, Kalapana, Big Island by John Penisten Photography

page 113: Cinder Cone, Mauna Kea, Big Island by John Penisten Photography

page 114: Kaneohe Bay, Kualoa Ridge and Chinaman's Hat by Ann Cecil, Stock Photos Hawaii

page 117: Demdrobium Orchids by John Penisten Photography

RECIPE CONTRIBUTERS

Patricia Caringella
Catering by Patricia Caringella
Lake Oswego, OR 97034
503.676.2952

Kahala Mandarin Oriental Hotel
5000 Kahala Avenue
Honolulu, HI 96815

Chai Chaowasaree
Singha Thai
1910 Ala Moana Boulevard
Honolulu, HI 96815

Laurent Poulain
Ritz-Carlton at Mauna Lani
1 North Kaniku Drive
Kohala Coast, HI 96743

Alejandro Fernandez
Outrigger Prince Kuhio Hotel
2500 Kuhio Avenue
Honolulu, HI 96815

Fenton Lee
Hyatt Regency
1571 Poipu Road
Koloa, Kauai, HI 96756

Fred Halpert
Brava Terrace
3010 St. Helena Hwy, North
St. Helena, CA 94574

Daphne Higa
Grand Wailea Resort
3850 Wailea Alanue
Wailea, Maui, HI 96753

Gerard Reversade
Gerard's at the Plantation Inn
174 Lahainaluna Road
Lahaina, Maui, HI 96761

Glenn Chu
Indigo Restaurant
1121 Nuuanu Avenue
Honolulu, HI 96817

Elizabeth Thomas
Elizabeth Thomas Cooking School
1372 Summit Road
Berkeley, CA 94708

Scott Lutey
Napili Kai Beach Club
5900 Honoapiilani
Lahaina, HI 96761

David Paul Johnson
David Paul's Lahaina Grill
127 Lahainaluna Road
Lahaina, Maui, HI 96761

Andre Fusero
Hawaii Prince Hotel Waikiki
100 Holomoana Street
Honolulu, HI 96815

Edward Frady
Edward's at Kanaloa
78-261 Manakai Street
Kailua-Kona, HI 96740

Kea Lani Hotel
4100 Wailea Alanui
Wailea, Maui, HI 96753

Stephen Marquard
Outrigger Marshall Island Resort
P.O. Box 3279
Majuro, MH 96960

Eileen Yin-Fei Lo
Author
33 Lloyd Road
Montclair, New Jersey 07042

Merriman's Restaurant
Box 2349
Kamuela, HI 96743

Catherine Whims
Genoa Restaurant
2832 S.E. Belmont Street
Portland, OR 97214

David Brown
Hilton Waikola Village
425 Waikola Beach Drive
Waikola, HI 96738

William Trask
The Ilikai Yacht Club Restaurant and Bar
1777 Ala Moana Boulevard
Honolulu, HI 96815

Index